W9-BVV-201

B
3776

# THURMAN ARNOLD, SOCIAL CRITIC

*The Satirical Challenge to Orthodoxy*

# THURMAN ARNOLD

# SOCIAL CRITIC

*The Satirical Challenge to Orthodoxy*

by EDWARD N. KEARNY

ALBUQUERQUE
UNIVERSITY OF NEW MEXICO PRESS

Excerpts from FAIR FIGHTS AND FOUL by Thurman Arnold are reprinted by permission of Harcourt, Brace & World, Inc.; © 1951, 1960, 1965 by Thurman Arnold.

© 1970 by the University of New Mexico Press. All rights reserved.
Manufactured in the United States of America.
Library of Congress Catalog Card No. 78-107099.
Designed by Bruce Gentry.
*First Edition*

TO MY PARENTS

# ACKNOWLEDGMENTS

I wish to express my appreciation to Dr. Robert Goostree of the American University School of Law; to Dr. Martin Meadows, Dr. Royce Hanson, and Dr. Jerome Hanus of the American University School of Government; and to Dr. Carlton Jackson of Western Kentucky University for offering helpful comments on my manuscript. I am also grateful for the cooperation extended me by the Department of Government of Western Kentucky University. My task was facilitated throughout by the encouragement and assistance of my wife, Mary Ann, and by the fine typing of Mrs. Helen Newhouse and Mrs. Deloris Hutton. Finally, I am grateful for having had the opportunity of spending a Sunday afternoon with Thurman Arnold discussing a wide range of topics.

# CONTENTS

# THURMAN ARNOLD, SOCIAL CRITIC

*The Satirical Challenge to Orthodoxy*

# INTRODUCTION

Thurman Wesley Arnold (1891–1969) was a state legislator, a small town mayor, a law school dean, a professor of law at Yale University, an Assistant Attorney General, a federal judge, and a prominent big city lawyer. He was also a highly gifted writer and thinker.

Richard Hofstadter, in *The Age of Reform,* has referred to Arnold's writings as "the most advanced of the New Deal camp." He believes that Arnold wrote "better books . . . than any of the political criticism of the Progressive era." It is somewhat surprising, in the light of this assessment, that Arnold has received only the briefest mention in most texts and broad treatises on American political thought. It is also surprising that there are no published secondary materials dealing comprehensively with Arnold's social and political thought. The purpose of this study is to provide a comprehensive survey of Arnold's writings and, in so doing, to focus attention on his contribution to American social and political thought.

Few modern social thinkers are as puzzling and at the same time as interesting as Thurman Arnold. Those who remember his courageous defense of government employees during the McCarthy period consider him a libertarian. Others—after reading portions of Arnold's *Folklore of Capitalism* (1937) or his *Symbols of Government* (1935)—find dangerous totalitarian tendencies in his writings. Arnold persuaded many scholars that he was a tough-minded realist who laughed at taking ideals seriously. To many conservatives who observed his antitrust campaigns, however, he seemed to be a single-minded and dangerous crusader.

Not being inclined toward self-analysis, Arnold did nothing to unravel the many contradictory images he managed to create for himself. Instead of apologizing for inconsistencies, he cheerfully admitted them and seemed to revel in being a puzzling personality. Unfortunately, students of American social thought have done little to dispel the confusion. The reason, I believe, is that evaluations of Arnold have been too hastily drawn from a cursory inspection of his two major works, *Symbols* and *Folklore*. These books are highlighted by a series of dramatic overstatements used by Arnold to drive his points home. To emphasize the irrational nature of political persuasion, for example, he suggested that the best form of government is that found in an insane asylum. Such statements are the first to be picked up by quotation collectors seeking to enliven secondary sources. A picture of Arnold as a cynical manipulator emerges, while his humanitarianism, social tolerance, and the consistent subthemes—such as gradual and nonviolent social change and peaceful coexistence of social interests—that point to his most enduring moral commitments are overlooked.

This study is based on the premise that a deeper understanding of Thurman Arnold as a social theorist can be gained by a careful presentation and analysis of more than three decades of his writings and speeches. In executing this task I have not attempted to present Arnold as a systematic thinker. I have, however, tried to organize the various elements of his writings in such a way as to show relationships which have been largely ignored by most of those who have commented on his books and articles.

The relationships within Thurman Arnold's writings are not the only focus of this study. It also examines Arnold's kinship to a group of late nineteenth- and early twentieth-century American thinkers to discover which elements of his thought were shared by earlier dissenters and which were *sui generis*. Common elements are stressed in the first two chapters and those which are unique are discussed in chapters III

4

through VI. My intent throughout this study has been to convey as accurately as possible the content and flavor of Arnold's many observations on American society. In so doing, I hope to provide a foundation for future evaluations of him as a perceptive and provocative American critic. I have taken the first step toward evaluation here. I hope there will be others.

CHAPTER I

# INTELLECTUAL DISSENT
# IN THE AGE OF ARNOLD

The philosophy of Thurman Arnold is not an isolated phenomenon. It is part of a larger American intellectual tradition of revolt against established systems of thought. Arnold's contribution to American political thought can be best understood in the context of this dissident tradition. From the late nineteenth century to the 1930s (when Arnold's most important writings appeared) criticism of both the methods and conclusions of traditional social thought was growing in extent and influence. The prominent intellectuals in all fields who formulated this criticism were rarely if ever identical in their approaches or conclusions. There was almost always an aspect of uniqueness in their contribution. Nevertheless, they were bound together, however loosely, by certain common characteristics which set them apart from established systems of thought.

6

The dissenters attacked the notion of absolute, universal, and unchanging ideas in all fields of social theory. They insisted, moreover, that these fields (law, economics, politics, and so forth) must be studied as inseparable parts of a larger social whole. The beliefs and practices of society were not logically derived from absolute principles, but were historical products of human experience. Historical analysis led them to the conclusion that the ideals of American society had not kept pace with its technological and organizational growth. The dissenters were proud of their detachment from the prevailing norms of society. Their writings, as Thurman Arnold expressed it, were intended to disturb the attitude of religious worship with a few practical observations.

It is not surprising that the formulation of new assumptions and approaches in social studies was accompanied by an emphasis on social criticism and reform. By destroying the insulation of traditional social ideas from the perspectives of history and a wide variety of other disciplines, dissenting thinkers opened new avenues for social criticism. By attacking the validity of universal and eternal ideas, the dissenters provided a more hospitable environment for social change and reform. They believed that reform could best be achieved by applying the scientific method to social problems.

The origin of these new ideas cannot be attributed to any one man or to any single area of social thought. A general reorientation in philosophy was needed to provide a framework as well as a stimulus for unorthodox thinking in particular fields. Such a reorientation began to crystallize in the early 1870s and culminated in the social philosophy of John Dewey. As it developed, this philosophical movement—which came to be known as "pragmatism"—mounted a general attack on absolute *a priori* ideas and became the most important expression of philosophical relativism in late nineteenth- and early twentieth-century America.

William James publicly credited his friend Charles Peirce (a mathematician and philosopher of logic) with the authorship of the doctrine of "practicalism or pragmatism." Peirce, however, insisted that pragmatism began, not with any single thinker, but with a *group* of thinkers. In the early 1870s, he recalls, "a knot of us young men in Old Cambridge" (including Peirce, William James, Chauncey Wright, John Fiske, and Oliver Wendell Holmes, Jr.) met frequently "to discuss fundamental questions." The group called itself "The Metaphysical Club."

7

*Thurman Arnold, Social Critic*

"It was there," states Peirce, "that the name and doctrine of pragmatism saw the light." [1]

The historical source of Peirce's definition of pragmatism was Kant's *Critique of Pure Reason*. A passage from his work illustrates the element in Kant's thought which appealed not only to Peirce but to the other members of The Metaphysical Club as well. Kant uses the term "pragmatic belief" to describe the probabilistic knowledge used by a doctor as his basis of action in diagnosing and treating a disease. In Kant's words, it is a "contingent belief which . . . forms the basis of the use of means for the attainment of certain ends." The great difference between the precursors of American pragmatism and Kant was the denial by the former of transcendent, rational, and absolute ideas existing over and above contingent pragmatic beliefs.[2]

The conception of ideas as contingent and changing, tied to scientific observation and geared to action, was a direct challenge to the notion of self-evident, unchanging, and absolute ideas. Even physical laws such as gravitation, Peirce contended, could not be considered immutable and eternal. They should be conceived as continuous with natural life-forms which are constantly evolving.[3] Peirce was talking about physical not social laws. Yet he was clearly eroding the foundations of orthodox social thought which was accustomed to demonstrating the immutability of established social ideas by comparing them to natural or physical laws. Peirce struck closer to the heart of conservative thought by stating that human ends are even more changeable than natural ends and more susceptible to conscious control. Although he was not attempting to fashion a liberal social philosophy, Peirce was providing an inviting framework for other pragmatic thinkers who wished to do so.

William James, through his writing and particularly through his extensive lecturing, became the great popularizer of pragmatism. Like Peirce, however, he had no strong interest in social theory. He credited his friend with starting him in the right philosophical direction—one which insisted that the effective meaning of any idea can always be brought down to some particular consequence in our practical experience.[4] Moreover, "truth" for James was too great for any one mind to comprehend, even if that mind is labeled "the absolute." The facts of life require many observers to take them in. For this reason, no point of view could be absolutely public and universal.[5] James did not extend his pragmatism to social theory because he looked to the individ-

8

ual rather than to legal, political, or economic institutions for social bet-
terment. When he protested against big business or imperialism, it was
as a morally indignant individualist, poorly informed about complex social conditions and the possible means of institutional change.[6] The
full-fledged application of the pragmatic method to social philosophy
awaited the seminal contribution of John Dewey.

The state of academic philosophy in 1879, when Dewey was an
undergraduate, was bleak. Philosophers distinguished themselves as defenders of those traditional principles existing "prior to and independent
of experience." G. Stanley Hall recalls that there were no more than
half a dozen colleges and universities in America where philosophy was
not tied to some theological formula.[7] Dewey was fortunate enough to
undertake his graduate studies in one of these, Johns Hopkins University. Its faculty included Charles Peirce who had already formulated the
outlines of his pragmatic position.

Unfortunately for intellectual historians who search for clear and neat
philosophical connections, Dewey did not discover Peirce until twenty
years later. His development was largely independent of the early "prag-
matists" who exchanged ideas as members of The Metaphysical Club in
Old Cambridge. At Hopkins, Dewey was drawn not to Peirce but to
George S. Morris, a devotee of the Hegelian school of German idealism.
The development of Dewey's pragmatic logic and his complete break
with idealism took place between 1891 and 1900 as a result of his work
in many fields outside philosophy—including ethics, psychology, and education. During this period, the concept of universal mind completely
dropped out of Dewey's writings and was replaced by the notion of
ideas as theoretical instruments for solving human problems.[8]

*Reconstruction in Philosophy,* written by Dewey in 1920, evidences
the author's intent to use pragmatic logic as a tool to transform social
philosophy. The task of philosophy, he contended, must be transferred
from the pursuit of fixed and universal ends to the detection of ills that
need remedy in a special case. Abstract philosophy has solved only abstract issues, leaving concrete problems exactly as they were before.
Thus, elaborate conceptions of "the state" and its relationship to "the
individual" have contented philosophers while completely ignoring the
problems of particular groups of individuals suffering in particular social
situations. Because intelligence has failed to come to grips with these
particular situations, the resolution of social problems is left to the crud-

9

est empiricism, shortsighted opportunism, and the matching of brute forces.[9]

Dewey insisted that until social ideas were judged by their consequences rather than celebrated as universal truths, intelligent social action and relief of social ills would be impossible. "I should indeed not hesitate to assert," he said, "that the sanctification of ready-made antecedent universal principles as methods of thinking is the chief obstacle to the kind of thinking which is the indispensable prerequisite of steady, secure and intelligent social reforms. . . ." [10]

The experimental method, which is the scientific judge of consequences, must be extended to social studies. The physical sciences, noted Dewey, were freed from the bondage of preconceived universal truths by the philosophers of the seventeenth century. The present need was to give similar freedom to social studies by extending the experimental method to them.

The implications of Dewey's philosophy were pervasive. In all fields of social study—economics, political science, sociology, law, or religion —he emphasized empiricism rather than absolutism, change rather than permanence, social reform rather than social apologetics. Eric Goldman has ably summarized Dewey's impact across the many fields of social science as follows:

> From Henry George to Charles Beard, reform thinkers had been feeling their way toward specific pragmatisms in their own fields . . . each had denied that the prevailing ideas could be eternally true, fixed by the nature of man and of the universe. Each had insisted that conservatism be tested by its political and economic results. . . . And now John Dewey had swept all their specific pragmatisms into a system from which each reformer, working away in his own field, could draw comfort and strength.[11]

Since the 1870s, a group of young economists had been feeling their way toward a more pragmatic conception of their own field. Some had received their doctorates from German universities where the classical economics prevailing in England and America was roundly criticized from a historical viewpoint. For Richard T. Ely, graduate study in Germany provided an "exhilarating atmosphere of freedom" which he had not experienced as an undergraduate in America. Economics at Columbia College (his alma mater) was regarded as a finished product. An undergraduate could become an economist by reading a single volume—

Mrs. Fawcett's *Political Economy for Beginners*. The text emphasized the unchanging economic laws governing production and distribution. Free competition was the most important law. If left alone by state and society, free competition would bring all economic relations into harmony. By Mrs. Fawcett's lights, the humanitarian relief societies which had been set up in Lancashire to aid jobless and starving Englishmen were "a most striking example of the harm that may be done by interfering with competition." [12]

Having tasted the "new and living economics" taught in the German universities, Ely and other young scholars were "depressed with the sterility of the old economics which was being taught in the American colleges . . . [and] determined to inject new life into American economics." The youthful determination expressed by Ely was to find concrete expression in 1885, when he and other reform-minded economists met in Saratoga Springs, New York, to form the American Economic Association. The Saratoga meeting produced a statement of principles which is a significant landmark in the development of American economics. It read in part:

> 1. We regard the state as an agency whose positive assistance is one of the indispensable conditions of human progress. . . .
> 2. We believe that political economy is still in an early stage of development . . . and we look, not so much to speculation as to historical and statistical study of actual conditions of economic life for the satisfactory accomplishment of that study.[13]

Several significant implications of this statement should be noted. It begins by a frontal assault on the *laissez faire* conclusions of orthodox economics and, by so doing, clears the way for acceptance of social reform. The second part of the statement constitutes a clear break with the assumptions and methods of orthodox economics. Political economy is *not* viewed as the secular manifestation of eternal economic laws, but as an ongoing process growing out of a concrete historical situation. Abstract speculation is distrusted as a method of study, while the perspective of history and the detachment of statistics are strongly recommended.

While the principles of the American Economic Association signified an important challenge to self-satisfied orthodoxy in economics, they were fairly mild compared to the devastating critique formulated by one of America's most eccentric and original thinkers—Thorstein Veblen.

As an undergraduate at Carleton College (1874–80) Veblen's introduction to economics was in much the same vein as Ely's experience at Columbia. All courses were taught as slightly variant branches of moral philosophy. Instructors were deemed capable of teaching any subject as long as "the light of godly example" radiated from their life and work. Students in economics used Reverend A. L. Chapin's 1878 "revision" of Bishop Francis Wayland's popular text of 1837. Economic principles being more or less permanent, Chapin could confidently state that "scarcely any changes have been made in the (earlier) opinions presented." The text conceived of economics as a "business science," man as an "exchanging being," and competition as a "beneficent, permanent law of nature." The higher principles of political economy were self-evident to those with common sense and an ability to understand the English language.[14]

Veblen, although a social and intellectual misfit, managed to graduate from Carleton in 1880. He proceeded to drift from institution to institution, teaching and studying. He earned his Ph.D. in philosophy at Yale in 1884, but his difficulties in securing and retaining teaching positions kept him drifting for the rest of his life. Between 1898 and 1900, Veblen put his critical intelligence to work in a series of articles published by *The Quarterly Journal of Economics*. He addressed himself to "The Preconceptions of Economic Science" and asked "Why is Economics not an Evolutionary Science?" His conclusions were an open challenge to economic orthodoxy. Man's view of life, contended Veblen, is a composite of two incompatible habits of thought. One is that of modern science which adheres to an impersonal cause-and-effect sequence and is materialistic and evolutionary in viewpoint. The other is the animistic point of view based on some preconceived form of natural law which is thought to determine the course of events, but which in reality simply reflects the dominant, commonsense ideals of conduct. The latter viewpoint prevails in American economics with its emphasis on the idea of an invisible hand of competition guiding economic relationships in a timeless continuum.[15]

Herbert Spencer's historical school of economics appears to be scientific but is actually prescientific in outlook. Like classical or orthodox economics, it identifies the normal state of affairs with the ideal. Spencerians employ a "conjectural history" narrating "what should have been" to buttress the preconceived ideal shared by classical economics;

i.e., that there should be no interference with competitive struggle in the economic order. It is no accident, concluded Veblen, that classical economists tend to be Spencerians.[16]

Orthodox economics in Veblen's day was truly a "business science" in the sense that its conclusions, with minor exceptions, gave strong support to the *laissez faire* ideology of America's industrialists. Spencer's "conjectural history" supplied the complementary doctrine of "survival of the fittest" in a competitive world. Veblen's reply was his own brand of anthropological history which had the effect of turning Spencer upside down. Whereas Spencer pictured the businessman as the vanguard of a progressive future, Veblen described him as the relic of a predatory past.

Veblen's critique appeared in 1899 with the publication of *The Theory of the Leisure Class*—widely regarded as his most important work.[17] The author concentrated on tracing what he considered to be the two basic features of modern society—industry and business—to their origins at the dawn of cultural history. In the earliest savage societies, observed Veblen, labor was divided into drudgery and exploit. These evolved, respectively, into industry and warfare in the barbarian world and finally into industry and business in the modern world. From the earliest era of drudgery to the modern era, industry has concerned itself with the productive and creative task of shaping inert materials for human use. However, because such work was relegated to women at the outset and because it lacked an adventurous show of strength, it never achieved the social prestige that was awarded to exploit, i.e., the hunt, war, and finally business.

The implication of Veblen's theory was that social prestige and control have been historically divorced from the quiet sources of human progress. He elaborated further on this theme in *The Theory of Business Enterprise* (1904).[18] In modern society technicians and engineers are responsible for and interested in industrial efficiency. Those engaged in business are far more concerned with obtaining control through buying, selling, and otherwise manipulating financial securities. The engineer becomes an expert in the methods of production, while the businessman becomes an expert in the movements of the securities market. Technicians are the creators of the material basis of prosperity, while businessmen are the masters of controlling it. The businessmen's control, however, tends to be erratic. Financial manipulations for profit frequently

13

disrupt the steady process of industrial production, causing unpredictable depressions.

In this fashion, Veblen diametrically opposed the enonomic logic of Herbert Spencer. To Spencer, the businessman was the *creator* of a prosperous economic system. To Veblen, as Robert Heilbroner has aptly expressed it, the businessman becomes the *saboteur* of the system.[19]

Although Veblen's writing was perhaps the most devastating critique of capitalism ever penned by a prominent American intellectual, he did not consider himself a social reformer. His motive, as he professed it, was "idle curiosity." It cannot be doubted, however, that the results of this eccentric professor's "idle curiosity" provided reformers with a very powerful intellectual weapon. As John Maurice Clark has observed, "[Veblen] more than any other man altered the course of American economic thought until the orthodoxy of yesterday is today the theory everyone is trying to overthrow, replace or modernize. . . . He may be taken as the largest personal impulse behind the modern critical movements. . . ."[20]

Veblen's denial of personal involvement in the issues he was discussing exemplifies his use of the anthropological-detached approach as a literary device. This detachment was not expressed in the patient collection of facts (as was the case with another prominent institutional economist, John R. Commons) or in the use of sophisticated statistical techniques (as was the case with Veblen's foremost intellectual heir, Wesley C. Mitchell) but in a speculative philosophy which dissected society without concern for offending prevailing social norms. Joseph Dorfman contends that "One of the most important facets of Veblen's character was his anthropological objectivity, which sharpened while it deepened his insights. He generally managed to write in the terse and impersonal manner of a man from another planet and prosaically dissected the pecuniary foundations of modern society."[21]

Veblen's original work provided a broad theoretical framework within which able colleagues and followers pursued "more intensive and tamer inquiries," as Wesley Mitchell phrased it. For this reason, Veblen is considered the originator of the "institutional" school of economics. Members of this school were bound together by the sharpness of their break from orthodoxy and by a broad similarity of approach. Professor Allan G. Gruchy has made a comprehensive study of the similarities uniting six leading institutional economists: Thorstein Veblen, John R.

Commons, Wesley C. Mitchell, John Maurice Clark, Rexford G. Tugwell, and Gardiner C. Means.[22] All these men moved toward philosophical relativism by rejecting fixed or universal economic ideas, were interested in the problem of philosophical lag, favored the holistic method of
investigation, and used an anthropological approach to formulate social
criticism and recommend reform.

The philosophic basis of American economics in the early twentieth
century was derived largely from the assumptions of eighteenth-century
physics. The universe was assumed to be an unchanging order whose operations could be reduced to a number of universal laws.[23] Orthodox
economics in America adopted a similar assumption that the economic
universe was an unchanging order governed by static universal laws. Institutional economics rejected this fundamental tenet by insisting that
rapid change was the most prominent characteristic of the modern
American economy.

In the static world of orthodox economics, there was little recognition of the lags between unchanging ways of thinking and rapidly evolving economic conditions.[24] The institutional economists, however, were
acutely aware of the problem of philosophical lag. This awareness led
them to abandon rationalistic economics in favor of an economics of adjustment. Habit, not reason, was to them the primary characteristic of
human thought and action. Habitual responses so often fell behind technological realities that man's central problem became adjustment to new
circumstances. The institutionalists noted that economic problems were
accumulating at a rate which far exceeded the rate of psychological adjustment on the part of the general population. They hoped, by their
writings and participation in public affairs, to facilitate the process of adjusting ideas to rapid economic change.

Holism is such a prominent aspect of institutional economics that
Professor Gruchy prefers to use the term "holistic economics" to describe this school. Its members insisted that economic events must be
considered as a part of a social and cultural whole. They urged economists to assimilate the findings of related disciplines to broaden their
own studies.

John R. Commons, for example, brought extensive legal and historical knowledge to bear on his analysis of the economic system. In *Legal
Foundations of Capitalism*,[25] he traced the changing conceptions of law
and property during the evolution of the British economy from feudal-

ism to modern capitalism. His analysis demonstrated that the public law of England was not static but a product of the changing practices of businessmen, guilds, and landlords. Commons proceeded to demonstrate the equally dynamic relationship between American law and property. His careful investigations of court decisions were not intended to master their legal logic but to understand the economic theories of judges who made decisions involving the allocation of millions of dollars.[26] Commons' theory of collective economic action was also holistic in approach, being based on impressive knowledge of the new thinking in a variety of fields. As Gruchy has observed, "It was not until he had assimilated much of the social philosophy of William James, the pragmatic psychology of John Dewey and the legal theories of the sociological jurists that Commons felt prepared to embark upon an exposition of . . . 'collective economics.' " [27]

The institutional economists attempted to view the American economy through the eyes of an anthropologist who would be unaffected by preconceived economic ideas. By moving the economic and cultural ideal of free competition to one side before observing the economy, the economists reached conclusions quite different from those of economic orthodoxy. At the center or core of the American economy, they found monopolistic or predominantly monopolistic enterprises. Business became more and more competitive as one moved toward the outer limits of the economy. The general character of the economy was influenced most by its monopolistic core which acted as a vortex drawing toward its center more and more of the nation's economic life.

The institutionalists observed that in the peripheral competitive areas of the economy there was a high degree of correspondence between money making and goods making, i.e., between profit and production. In the monopolistic areas of the economy, however, profit was less a reward for producing goods than for restricting output, creating artificial scarcities, and securing protection from the leveling influences of competitive forces.[28] Thus, by detaching their observations from the ideal of free competition, they were led to reject the orthodox notion of natural harmony between profit and production.

The followers of Thorstein Veblen were much more willing than he was to make proposals for reform. John R. Commons and Wesley Mitchell, in different ways, set the most important precedents in both action and thought for later reform-minded economists such as Rexford

Tugwell. Commons' major social concern was with legally secured rights for workingmen. This led him to serve on numerous public bodies including President McKinley's Industrial Commission, the Wisconsin Industrial Commission, and the U.S. Commission on Industrial Relations. His reform interests, however, ranged far and wide. In 1923, with Professors Ripley and Fetter, he represented four Western states before the Federal Trade Commission in a case involving price discrimination by the U.S. Steel Corporation. He organized and directed the Bureau of Economy and Efficiency of the City of Milwaukee from 1911–13. Another reform outlet for Commons was his frequent appearance before Congressional committees. Perhaps his most important testimony was in support of Senator Robert La Follette's bill for the physical valuation of the railways by the Interstate Commerce Commission. Commons' cooperation with La Follette had begun in 1905 when the latter was governor of Wisconsin. At the governor's request, Commons drafted a civil service law and later a public utility law for the state of Wisconsin.[29]

The importance of John R. Commons as a reformer was enormously increased by his ability to inspire outstanding students. Kenneth Boulding has observed that through these students "Commons was the intellectual origin of the New Deal, of labor legislation, of social security, of the whole movement in this country towards a welfare state." Although his operations were mostly confined to Wisconsin, he was "the first brain truster . . . setting a pattern of great importance for the next generation." [30]

Like Commons, Wesley Mitchell was an early brain truster with extensive service to government as researcher, consultant, and planner. As early as 1918, Mitchell was urging the national government to improve its statistical and planning operations so that policy might be more closely tied to quantitative knowledge. He served on a series of national planning agencies, beginning with President Hoover's Committee on Social Trends. The recommendations of this committee helped pave the way for other planning agencies established after 1933, including the National Resources Planning Board on which Mitchell served in 1934–35.[31]

Wesley Mitchell's conception of reform was heavily influenced by the pragmatism of John Dewey. It is doubtful that any of the dissenting intellectuals of the late nineteenth and early twentieth centuries made a more faithful attempt to implement Dewey's concept of applied social intelligence than did Mitchell. He took the lead among the dissenters in developing sophisticated statistical techniques for the purpose of creating and sharpening social intelligence. His participation on various national planning agencies reflects an effort to *apply* scientific intelligence to social problems—to give concrete expression to Dewey's ideal of social intelligence at work. Mitchell shared Dewey's preference for planned reconstruction over piecemeal reform. Other dissenters, notably Thurman Arnold, were more inclined to adjust the pragmatic method to the conflicting currents of politics, where piecemeal changes seemed a more realistic objective.

The character and impact of institutional economics were accurately described by John Maurice Clark when he compared Veblen's work with orthodox economic theory. The latter, he thought, was a "deductive static economics" which was erected on the "assumption of contentment." Veblen's economics sought to explore the process of economic change and, unlike orthodox theory, was an economics of discontent.[32]

Dissident economics in the late nineteenth and early twentieth centuries was closely related to the newly developing field of sociology. The birth of sociology as a separate field of study was largely an expression of the desire to broaden the perspective of established disciplines, particularly economics. Charles Horton Cooley, for example, received his doctorate in economics in 1894. Soon afterward, he moved into sociology, then in its infancy, to subject his economic notions to a broader type of criticism.[33]

The treatment of economics in standard textbooks, Cooley thought, was narrowly confined to an elaboration of economic mechanism with scant attention given to the wider social and economic significance of the mechanism. He attempted to make economic concepts more realistic by subjecting them to a broad social analysis. The concept of "demand," for example, could not be uncritically accepted as a starting point of economic analysis. Viewed from a social perspective, demand was "an expression of economic power . . . as determined by all the existing conditions." Viewed from a historical perspective, it was part of man's inheritance, flowing into the present like "a turbid stream, bearing with it all those struggles and compromises that make up human history." Uncritical acceptance of "demand" as a starting point of economic analysis led to uncritical acceptance of the economic system, for, as Cooley noted, "All the evils of the economic system, except those which are added in the market process, are already implicit in demand, and of course are transmitted to production and distribution." [34]

Cooley's broad holistic approach was an important influence on a rising group of liberal economists who read his writings and came into personal contact with him. Walton Hale Hamilton, an institutional economist who later became a colleague of Thurman Arnold's on the Yale Law School faculty, noted that Cooley ". . . led us away from an atomistic individualism, made us see 'life as an organic whole,' and revealed to us 'the individual' and 'society' remaking each other in an endless process of change." [35]

A second sociologist who was also closely related to the new trends in economics was Edward A. Ross. He had done his graduate work at Johns Hopkins among the German-trained rebels in economics including Richard T. Ely. Ross's development is a clear example of pioneer sociology growing out of a discontent with orthodox economics, both classical and Spencerian. Ross began his teaching career using Spencer's *Sociology*. From the beginning he doubted the author's distinction between the voluntarism of business and the compulsory nature of the state. After three years, Ross informed Lester Ward, "I have finally cut loose from Spencer for he has become so unsatisfactory it is no pleasure to put him in the hands of students." [36] One year later, Ross was beginning to feel the excitement of being part of a sociological movement against economic orthodoxy: "The interest in Sociology is certainly growing among economists. . . . Think of it. The other day I found myself (referring to Spencer) compelled to use the phrase 'classical sociology.' Soon we shall have the 'old school' and the 'new school' and all the rest." [37]

Ross's opinion of the classical economics of Adam Smith and Ricardo was also critical. "Neither of these men," he observed, "make any declarations about social philosophy. They confined themselves in the most rigid way to a study of wealth. They did not compare competition with cooperation because . . . there was so little of the latter that they could conceive of nothing else than competiton." [38] After eleven years of pioneering in sociology, Ross was more aware than ever of the challenge his developing field was posing to the champions of economic orthodoxy:

> I am beginning to see that the campaign in disparagement of sociology and the reluctance of some of the big institutions to meet the demand for sociological instruction is not due entirely to the

errors of the sociologists but in part to the deadly enmity of sociology to the *laissez faire*, "natural rights," "freedom of contract" philosophy which is one of the bulwarks of vested interests.[39]

Ross fully shared Cooley's holistic conception of sociology. The notion that society could be neatly divided into separate fields of study was based on false assumptions. If it were true, argued Ross, that each human craving generated in society certain creeds, activities, and institutions which remained unmixed with the collective manifestations of other cravings, then there could be separate independent bodies of knowledge, each representing a particular human craving. Economics would explore the craving for wealth; politics, the craving for power; jurisprudence, the craving for justice, and so on. Unfortunately, this assumption, so often made by orthodox theory, is incorrect. "So far as specific cravings exist," contended Ross, "they react upon and modify one another. . . . They are trimmed and adjusted to fit into a plan of life." [40] Progress cannot be expected in fields which start from outworn assumptions: "The disciples of the abstract political economy, the unhistorical jurisprudence, the *a priori* ethics, and the speculative politics make no headway because they shut their eyes to the interdependence of dissimilar social facts." [41]

"Society," concluded Ross in a holistic vein, "no longer falls apart into neat segments like a peeled orange. State, law, religion, art, morals, industry, instead of presenting so many parallel streams of development, are studied rather as different aspects of *one social evolution*." [42]

Cooley and Ross shared a broad general approach, but they differed widely in both emphasis and personality. Cooley concerned himself primarily with the relationship of the individual to society. He strongly emphasized the subjective aspects of this interaction, e.g., individual motives, attitudes, and self-consciousness. In sharp contrast to Cooley's subjectivism, Ross concentrated on social forces, e.g., public opinion, law, ceremony, and social suggestion. Moreover, he was far more interested in social problems and social reform than was Cooley. These differences largely reflected the personalities of the men. Cooley was a quiet, introspective scholar; Ross was a confident, combative extrovert possessing a formidable 6-foot-6-inch, 250-pound frame.[43] Ross was not at all out of character when he rose and proclaimed to a quiet meeting of the American Sociological Society that there might "come a time in the career of every sociologist when it is his solemn duty to raise hell."

Edward Ross actually played two roles, that of the detached socio-logical theorist [44] and that of the social critic and reformer. He never, however, advocated a rigid separation of these roles. The aim of sociology, he asserted, "should be to bring to bear upon the outstanding social difficulties of our time the best possible techniques of inquiry." [45]

One great difficulty of the times at the turn of the century was the lag between the ethical ideals of society and modern social conditions. In response to this problem, Ross wrote a small but influential book entitled *Sin and Society*. His central thesis was that Americans were vividly aware of the old traditional sins but failed to recognize the new ones that had accompanied social change. "They do not see that . . . tax-dodging is larceny, that railroad discrimination is treachery, that the factory labor of children is slavery, that deleterious adulteration is murder." [46] Ross proudly identified his book with the muckraking literature of the time. Without "the literature of exposure," he contended, America would have suffered a "futile blowup . . . followed by iron military repression." Instead, thanks to the muckrakers, America got a healthy dose of reform legislation.[47]

William F. Ogburn, a younger sociologist, had much in common with Cooley and Ross. As a teacher of economics, history, political science, statistics, and sociology, he could not help but share their interdisciplinary interests. Ogburn's earliest publications, including his doctoral dissertation, were in the field of social legislation and the politics of democracy. Concentration on these topics reflected his early interest in social action and reform. However, academic training inculcated a more detached stance that led him to appraise the difficulties of achieving reform by direct legislation. An activist interest in social reform evolved into a scientific interest in social problems. This change, however, did not remove him from the scene of public service which included assignments as consultant to the National Recovery Administration, the National Resources Committee, and the Bureau of the Census.[48]

One of Ogburn's most important contributions to sociology was his concept of "cultural lag." This phenomenon occurs when one part of two correlated parts of culture changes before or in greater degree than the other part does, thereby causing social maladjustment. Ogburn cited as an example the maladjustment between the static laws dealing with industrial accidents and the rapidly changing machinery used in industry. He noted that, before the factory system, machines consisted of simple tools to which the common law of accidents was well suited. The industrial revolution, however, introduced whirling machinery with rapidly moving parts. Despite increased danger to the worker, accidents continued to be dealt with under the old common law. The result was social maladjustment observable in the form of frequent accidents followed by long delays in settlement and small compensation for workers injured or killed, leaving fatherless families. It was not until about 1910 that employers' liability and workmen's compensation laws were adopted in America, ending a cultural lag that had spanned four decades.[49]

Ogburn's illustration of cultural lag indirectly depicts a failure of social ideas to keep abreast of technological change. When illustrating cultural lag, Ogburn almost always featured technological change as the independent variable and nontechnical phenomena (ideas, laws, and so forth) as the lagging dependent variables. This characteristic makes it appropriate to consider his concept of cultural lag as another expression of the interest shown by many other dissenting thinkers in philosophical lag.[50]

Sociology and economics were not the only fields in which new developments were occurring. During the early twentieth century, the critical anthropological method was applied to the study of politics and government. The very frame of government, the Constitution, came under critical scrutiny. To conservatives who viewed the document as the embodiment of an immutable higher law, such scrutiny was almost sacrilegious. In 1879, E. J. Phelps, the newly elected president of the American Bar Association, proclaimed to his colleagues that the Constitution was too sacred to be discussed by nonlawyers. He did not think it was meant to be "hawked about the country, debated in the newspapers, discussed from the stump, elucidated by pot-house politicians and dunghill editors, scholars in the science of government who have never found leisure for the grace of English grammar. . . ."[51]

An explosion inevitably occurred in 1913 when younger defenders of the Phelps doctrine were informed of the publication of Charles Beard's *An Economic Interpretation of the Constitution of the United States*. The author had produced the most controversial work of his generation by asserting that the men who wrote America's higher law "were, with a few exceptions, immediately, directly, and personally interested in, and desired economic advantages from, the establishment of the new system."[52]

Charles Beard's career as a history professor at Columbia coincided with the progressive era in national politics. The muckrakers had popularized exposure of misdeeds in high places, and Theodore Roosevelt had used the White House as a "bully pulpit" to issue denunciations of the "malefactors of great wealth." [53]

Beard rode the tide of muckraking and progressivism, but his purpose was broader than those of the indignant journalists and progressive politicians of his day. He hoped to introduce a new mode of critical thinking to replace the old habits of uncritical reverence. As Hofstadter has observed, Beard was part of an emerging critical intelligentsia in the United States—men who rebelled against absolute ideas by asserting "that all things are related, that all things change, and that all things should therefore be explained historically rather than deductively." [54] Beard's particular passion was for searching out the hard realities which lie beneath lofty theories and ideals, the national ideal of the U.S. Constitution not excepted.

Although Beard became the most controversial critic of the Constitution and its revered authors, he was not the first. In 1907, J. Allen Smith had depicted the Constitution as a document designed to frustrate democracy, written by men with little sympathy for popular government.[55] Smith's book was widely read, particularly by progressives, but he revealed very little that was new or surprising. Conservatives since the Federalist era had agreed with Smith's conclusions and applauded the Founding Fathers for their healthy distrust of democracy. Smith was simply restating a time-worn generalization, hoping in a reform-minded era to produce a negative reaction. His book was almost entirely a *political* critique of the Constitution, leaving the area of *economic* interpretation wide open.[56]

With the predictability of a knee reflex, socialist historians A. M. Simons and Gustavus Myers reacted by placing great emphasis on the economic class interests of the framers. Liberal scholars, however, were not enthusiastic about criticisms tainted by associations with Marxist theory.[57] Beard was no doubt encouraged by the fact that his Columbia colleague, E. R. A. Seligman, had published a nonsocialist *Economic Interpretation of History* in 1902. The author dissociated his work from Marx's specific doctrine of the inevitable destruction of capitalism while at the same time asserting that economic forces are central to historical development.[58] Professor Seligman's thesis seemed to Beard "as nearly axiomatic as any proposition in social science can be." [59]

The sociological jurisprudence of Roscoe Pound helped to focus critical attention on the *judicial* process. A Columbia colleague of Beard's, F. J. Goodnow, further delimited the target of scrutiny in his book *Social Reform and the Constitution* (1911). Beard noted in the first chapter of his *Economic Interpretation* that "almost the only indication of a possible economic interpretation to be found in current American jurisprudence is implicit in the writings of a few scholars like Roscoe Pound and Professor Goodnow, and in occasional opinions rendered by Mr. Justice Holmes. . . ." [60] In Goodnow's view, a virtually unamendable eighteenth-century Constitution interpreted by wholly unamenable judges blocked the passage of badly needed twentieth-century reforms. [61]

Beard undoubtedly shared Goodnow's contention that blind Constitution worship had joined hands with standpat conservatism in a holy war against reform. It seems likely that a strong dose of progressive indignation, combined with a desire to encourage critical objectivity, was the driving force behind Beard's controversial interpretation of the Constitution.

In the first chapter of his book, Beard opens with an attack on Bancroft's thesis that the adoption of the Constitution represented "the movement of the divine power which gives unity to the universe. . . ." [62] The whole people of the nation, without reference to economic interests, prepared the new document "by calm and friendly councils . . . in the happy morning of their existence. . . ." They had "chosen justice for their guide . . . [and] all the friends of mankind invoked success on their endeavor as the only hope for renovating the life of the civilized world." [63]

In place of Bancroft's inspiring prose, Beard presented "economic biographies" (based largely on U.S. Treasury records formerly ignored) of each of the fifty-five members attending the Constitutional Convention in 1787. Beard's data detailed the property holdings of each delegate—showing how these holdings would rise in value as a result of the adoption of the new Constitution. The great majority of the framers, he concluded, stood to gain financially from the new government they were creating.

Beard's economic interpretation of the Constitution diametrically opposed Bancroft's at every point. According to Beard, the Constititution was

(1) An economic document, supported mainly by bankers, holders

of public securities, land speculators, merchants, and manufacturers. The opposition came mainly from small farmers and debtors who saw the new document as a threat to their economic interests.

(2) Not ratified by the "whole people." About three-fourths of the adult males failed to vote due to indifference or disfranchisement because of property qualifications.[64]

The tone of dogmatic certainty in Beard's book represented a departure from the less dogmatic approach of other dissenting intellectuals. In view of the more perceptive criticisms of his work—including those from sympathetic historians—Beard would have done well to qualify his bold assertions.[65] In other respects, however, Beard's writing had much in common with other American dissenters. Like Thorstein Veblen, he wrote with the dispassionate air of scientific objectivity which nevertheless—and not by accident—made deep cuts into conservative ideology. Just as the institutional economists had undermined the notion of unchanging economic laws, so Beard had cast doubt on the belief that the Constitution was an immutable higher law unaffected by changing economic interests.

The anthropological approach was not confined to the study of the Constitution, but extended across the entire area of government and politics. The new political scientists shared Beard's passion for casting aside abstractions and studying the realities so often obscured or ignored by them. Political philosophy had been moving in two equally fruitless directions which they had no desire to follow. One was the path of pure speculation leading to supernatural or metaphysical theories of the state. The other was legal analysis which placed political theory under the bondage of lawyers. Both approaches gave to the political state an "air of abstraction and unreality" by ignoring the historical forces and social pressures underlying it.[66]

Dissenters in political science contended that close observation of the operations of government and politics was far more valuable than abstract theories of the state. Their studies led them from rational philosophy to irrational public opinion; from metaphysical notions of the state to party organizations, patronage systems, political bosses, and pressure groups. Arthur F. Bentley, a prominent figure among the early dissenters, insisted that *a priori* ideas be banished from the study of politics: "If we start with a theory about ideas and their place in politics, we are destroying our raw material even before we take a good peep at it. We are substituting something else which . . . will certainly color our entire further progress, if progress we can make at all on scientific lines." [67]

Bentley proclaimed a thoroughgoing philosophical relativism in political science. Just as Karl Marx had given meaning to ideas only as expressions of class interest, so Bentley gave meaning to ideas only as expressions of group interest. As he boldly put it: "Indeed the only reality of the ideas is their reflection of the groups, only that and nothing more. The ideas can be stated in terms of groups; the groups never in terms of the ideas." [68] Bentley's self-assured, monistic explanation of politics in terms of group conflict resembles Charles Beard's unqualified interpretation of the Constitution in terms of conflict between economic classes. Both men tended to replace traditional dogmatisms with new ones of their own making. In this respect, they were different from John Dewey and the institutional economists who avoided new as well as old dogmatisms.

Little was left of the notion of a fixed "law above men" after its dissection by Bentley. It was possible, he said, to cut through the dialectics of the Supreme Court's legal reasoning "till we get down to the actual groups of men underlying the decisions and producing the decisions through the differentiated activity of the justices." [69]

Other characteristics of the new political science appeared in the writings of Charles Merriam, a contemporary of Bentley's. He shared the broad holistic perspective of the institutional economists viewing institutions as "action patterns reaching into psychology, biology, sociology, philosophy, ethics, anthropology, economics, geography, science, and technology. . . ." [70] Leonard White later recalled Merriam leading his students "through a bold and persistent effort to marry political science with biology, anthropology, psychology, sociology, economics and medicine. This polygamous venture repelled many of the profession, but it intrigued the younger generation." [71] Merriam was attempting to free political science from its *exclusive* moorings in law and history. This did not imply an intention on his part to minimize the historical dimension of government and politics. "The study of government," he said, "might be based upon observation and analysis of *current* manipulations of various sorts, but a deeper study requires attention to the *evolutionary* quality of political effort and achievement. . . ." [72]

Like dissenters in many other fields, Merriam was disturbed by the failure of social thought to keep abreast of scientific advance. In the field of machine technology, he observed, "tradition is cast to the winds

. . . there is no boasting . . . that a machine is old, but that it is the newest and latest to be found. . . ." American industry had quickly accepted new ideas in technology, but held fast to an older (*laissez faire*) ideology to protect itself from regulation.[73]

To remedy modern economic and political maladjustments which he considered to be "of the most formidable and menacing type," Merriam took part in a long series of reform movements for responsible and efficient municipal government, zoning, party reform, the direct primary, the merit system, state constitutional reform, school reform, and national and regional planning. At the age of thirty-six, he was a candidate for mayor of Chicago. He served as an elected member of the City Council for six years.[74]

Merriam's philosophy of social reform was strongly pragmatic in spirit, emphasizing the application of scientific intelligence to social problems. "The finger of science," he asserted, "does not tremble as it points in the direction of conscious control of evolution." [75] Scientific control implied comprehensive social planning at all levels of government. Merriam denied that this would be an arbitrary or autocratic process. He envisioned democratic planning as a general scheme of regulation recognizing and protecting "areas of self-activity into which the state will not ordinarily penetrate." Merriam hoped to coordinate national and local policies, public, quasi-public, and private plans, instead of allowing them to drift apart or pull against each other.[76] As a strong advocate of social planning, it is not surprising that Merriam's public career coincided at several points with that of economist Wesley Mitchell. Both served on President Hoover's Research Committee on Social Trends in 1930 and, four years later, on President Roosevelt's National Resources Planning Board.

Dissenting intellectuals in the legal profession joined political scientists in the social dissection of law, the Constitution, and the Supreme Court. Oliver Wendell Holmes, Jr., was an early and prominent member of this group. Just as the institutional economists had rejected the notion that economic reality could be logically deduced from unchanging universal principals, so Holmes rejected the similar notion of the logical derivation of law. As early as 1881 he stated:

> The life of the law has not been logic: it has been experience. The felt necessities of the time, the prevalent moral and political theories, intuitions of public policy . . . even the prejudices which

judges share with their fellow-men, have had a good deal more to do than the syllogism in determining the rules by which men should be governed.[77]

The law, in other words, is mainly an expression of the practical experiences and changing beliefs of a people. To view it as pure logic or as something eternal ignores the obvious fact that law, like other secular phenomena, evolves in history. It "embodies the story of a nation's development through many centuries, and it cannot be dealt with as if it contained only the axioms and corollaries of a book of mathematics. In order to know what it is, we must know what it has been." [78] When Holmes emphasized the importance of understanding law from a historical perspective, he was not encouraging reverence for tradition but critical evaluation of it. The official theory of law, he observed, regarded precedents with reverence. Yet viewed historically, they frequently resemble the "clavicle in the cat" surviving long after the use they once served is ended.[79]

Holmes's most serious sin against orthodox legal theory was his determination to unveil the role of human bias in what was traditionally regarded as the impersonal process of judging, i.e., the task of mechanically applying, by impersonal logic, the dictates of a higher law to concrete cases. Holmes countered this view with a very unsettling assertion: " . . . the growth of the law is legislative . . . what the courts declare to have always been the law is in fact new. The very considerations which judges most rarely mention are the secret root from which the law draws all the juices of life. I mean, of course, considerations of what is expedient for the community concerned." [80]

Holmes did not abandon his penchant for detached analysis of the judicial function when he reached the august bench of the United States Supreme Court. His famous dissenting opinion in *Lochner* v. *New York* cut through the dialectics of the majority opinion to expose its economic foundation. "The case," he said, "is decided upon an economic theory which a large part of the country does not entertain." He reminded his fellow justices that it was not their duty to enact the *laissez faire* economics of Herbert Spencer into constitutional law.[81]

Like the prominent dissector of economic institutions, Thorstein Veblen, Holmes was not a social reformer. Nevertheless, his writings provided a powerful intellectual weapon for the reform minded. Holmes was an inspiration for many other socioeconomic thinkers, realists, and iconoclasts who, in diverse ways, called for legal reform.

Perhaps the most prominent of these was Roscoe Pound, the father of what came to be known as "sociological jurisprudence." Pound's image as a dissenter blossomed in what unexpectedly became a historic address before the American Bar Association in 1906. Pound, then in his early thirties, was the first law teacher to address the association.[82] Professor Wigmore, who was in the audience, recalls that the legal profession in 1906 "was a complacent, self-satisfied, genial fellowship of individual lawyers—unalive to the shortcomings of justice, unthinking of the urgent demands of the impending future . . . unaware of their collective duty. . . ." In such a contented atmosphere, the very topic Pound had chosen was disturbing—"The Causes of Popular Dissatisfaction with the Administration of Justice." Many of the old-timers scanning the program murmured, "Do we not give them a good enough justice? Whose idea can it be that things are wrong? Well, we are here; so we might as well stay and listen politely." [83]

As Pound began to speak, most of the lawyers sensed that they were listening to "a reform-wolf in sheep's clothing." Suspicion turned to alarmed indignation when the speaker hammered away at specifics: "Our procedure is behind the times. . . . The court's time is frittered away on mere points of legal etiquette. . . . Putting the courts into politics has almost destroyed the traditional respect for the Bench." [84] Most reactions to Pound's address were predictably hostile. "A more drastic attack upon the system of procedure," commented James Andrews of New York, "could scarcely be devised." Our system of procedure, he insisted, "is the most refined and scientific system ever devised by the wit of man." [85]

One year before Pound gave his unsettling address to the American Bar Association, *Foundations of Sociology* by Edward A. Ross had been published. The author predicted the inevitable decline of isolated, self-sufficient fields of social study and advocated a master science of society drawing on and integrating the significant findings of all the other social sciences. Pound and other legal thinkers became convinced that these ideas had much to offer the science of law.[86] The jurist's conviction of the self-sufficiency of jurisprudence had brought bad results. Among them, according to Pound, were: "the backwardness of the law in meeting social ends, the tardiness of lawyers in admitting or even perceiving such ends, and the gulf between legal thought and popular thought on matters of social reform which was so marked in the first decade of the present century." [87]

The subject matter of law in Pound's opinion had been confined too long to legal cases and judicial opinions. It must be broadened, he thought, to include a scientific understanding of the relationship of law to society—its interests and its problems. Pound described "sociological jurisprudence" as a pragmatic philosophy of law, stressing "the adjustment of principles and doctrines to the human conditions they are to govern rather than to assumed first principles." [88]

While the skeptical Holmes had left the process of adjustment to a clash of wills under democratic rules, Pound argued that the judges must creatively shape law to the social needs of the day. This "social engineering" aspect of Pound's thought was eagerly seized upon and employed more boldly by a group of thinkers who came to be known as "legal realists." Karl Llewellyn, a leading exponent of legal realism, acknowledged that Pound's writings formed "the basis of our forward-looking thought of the '20's and '30's and . . . provided half of the commonplace equipment on and with which our work since has builded." Unfortunately, he added, Pound's "brillant buddings have in the main not come to fruition." [89] The realists made it clear that they expected more from sociological jurisprudence than moderate reforms. They embraced the notion of judicial legislation with few qualms and faulted Pound for not accepting it unreservedly as the means of implementing his own ideas.[90]

A closely related dispute between Pound and the realists concerned their respective attitudes toward established legal rules. Pound, who had attacked uncritical adherence to rigid rules regardless of social considerations, still retained a large measure of respect for rules and precedents as guides for judges and stabilizers of the judicial process. The realists, on the other hand, regarded the judge's personal reaction to the facts of the case as the all-important determinant of its outcome. Rules were mainly rationalizations for preexisting biases. Accurate prediction of judicial behavior would be achieved only by emphasizing the extralegal factors influencing the decision.

The legal realists, therefore, turned eagerly to the social sciences for a true understanding of the judicial process. Professor Underhill Moore of the Yale Law School attempted to correlate cultural modes of behav-

ior with judicial behavior.[91] Jerome Frank and Edward S. Robinson analyzed legal institutions from a psychological standpoint. William O.
Douglas emphasized the impact of social and economic facts upon legal
doctrines.[92] Leon Green viewed legal philosophy as "a philosophy of
the total social organism of which law is only one phase." [93]

The link between Thurman Arnold's philosophy and the school of
legal realism is clear and direct. Professors Underhill Moore, Edward S.
Robinson, and William O. Douglas were all Arnold's colleagues at the
Yale Law School. Arnold has stated that his *Symbols of Government*
was an outgrowth of a seminar for law students given by himself and
Professor Robinson. William O. Douglas interested Arnold in serving
briefly as a trial examiner for the Securities and Exchange Commission.
This experience provided the basis for Arnold's second important book,
*The Folklore of Capitalism.*

A fourth colleague of Arnold's at the Yale Law School, Walton Hale
Hamilton, is difficult to classify as a member of a particular school. His
career united the tradition of legal dissent with the critical perspective of
institutional economics. Before his appointment as a professor of law at
Yale, Hamilton was a distinguished teacher and writer in economics,
and a strong advocate of the institutional approach. At Yale he did a
great deal to give substance to the effort of the law school to integrate
the study of law with the other social sciences.[94]

Hamilton, representing a confluence of dissenting forces, and being a
colleague of Arnold's, can be viewed as a concluding link in the loose
chain of dissent that leads to Arnold. The common characteristics of the
thinkers within this dissenting tradition—philosophical relativism, anthropological perspective, historicism, holism, interest in philosophical
lag and ideology, conclusions couched in terms of social criticism and reform—are closely interrelated and mutually reinforcing. The combined
impact of all these new ways of thinking about society posed a serious
challenge both to the methods and to the conclusions of established systems of social thought.

Recent dissident thought in America cannot be fully understood in
terms of its scholarly methods and conclusions alone. The emotional and
normative forces which impelled dissent must also be considered. The
impelling force most commonly found among the dissenting thinkers
considered in this chapter is an ethical-humanitarian impulse, frequently
religious in spirit. This impulse, while common, is by no means univer-

sally found among the dissenters. There is little evidence of it, for example, in the "tough-minded" philosophies of Holmes and Bentley. On the other hand, there is abundant evidence of it in the philosophy of Thurman Arnold, who was also sometimes referred to as "tough minded."

The humanitarian impulse was an important motivating force behind the "new school" of economics. It was no mere coincidence that the group of scholars who met at Saratoga Springs in 1885 to form the American Economic Association included Washington Gladden, a pioneer in the social gospel movement. Richard T. Ely, one of the founders of the association, was also a noted writer for church audiences. He authored *Social Law of Service* in which he asserted that "our exaltation is the exaltation of our fellows, their elevation is our enlargement." The ideal of social solidarity was not viewed as an accommodation of individual interests, but a unity whose expression was human brotherhood. In *Ground Under Our Feet,* Ely applied religious ethics to concrete situations such as child labor, female labor injurious to family life, Sunday labor, public corruption, and the need for recreational facilities in the cities. The author estimated that most Methodist ministers of his generation were influenced by these books to some degree.[95] Ely joined with another prominent dissenter in economics, John R. Commons, to organize the American Institute of Christian Sociology in 1893. The purpose of the institute was to encourage Americans to study social questions from both the scientific and the Christian standpoint.[96]

The ethical-humanitarian spirit of Ely and Commons was shared by the prominent sociologist, Charles H. Cooley. He criticized established economic theory for ignoring the important role of philanthropy and ethics. A social science which was not also "an ethical science," he said, "was unfaithful to its deepest responsiblility." [97] Humanitarianism appears even more strongly in the sociology of Edward A. Ross. The pragmatic Ross had no enthusiasm for theology which he described as "a sky-scraper founded on cobwebs." Yet he retained a deep respect for the ethical message of Christianity: "Will the *social idea* ever again be so beautifully set forth as it is in the Gospels? . . . The great churches," he said, "embody too much time-tested humanism not to take a hand in our own inescapable struggle against the unfolding . . . knaveries of capitalism." [98]

Ross considered "social religion" to be the noblest—if not the dominant or the most widespread—mechanism of social control. It is a product of spontaneous sympathy, not of intellect, force, or illusion. As expressed by Jesus, it proclaims "the union of all men in the bonds of an ideal brotherhood." [99] Social religion would always be a necessary element in reform. Social science might suggest directions, but the stimulus for reform must come from spontaneous sympathy. Social religion, Ross believed, could withstand theological revolutions—which do not strike at its humanistic foundations. "The only deadly and implacable foe of religious anthropology," he concluded, "is a positive or naturalist's way of looking upon man." [100]

The ethical humanitarian impulse in social thought was not confined to men like Ely, Commons, Cooley, and Ross, who openly expressed it, but also played an important, if disguised, part in shaping the thought of Thorstein Veblen. The ethical aspect of Veblen's thought appears most clearly in his theory of "instincts." He spoke of four instincts, two of which he labeled the "parental" instinct and the "acquisitive" instinct. The first of these originates with parental concern for one's offspring, and broadens to include a desire for the well-being of the tribe, the nation, and even mankind in general. The "parental" instinct is the opposite of the "acquisitive" instinct which leads the individual to take thought of his own personal welfare as contrasted with the welfare of others.[101]

Community definitions of status, thought Veblen, determine which human instincts will be most encouraged. He predicted a future struggle for dominance between the serviceable view of status (encouragement of the parental and workmanship instincts) and the predatory view of status (encouragement of the acquisitive instinct). The dominance of the former will foster technological progress and raise the living standards of the masses. The dominance of the latter will result in retardation of these goals.[102]

It is difficult to believe that a man who was morally indifferent, as Veblen claimed to be, could formulate an essentially ethical question in such an imaginative way. Perhaps one aspect of Veblen's genius was his remarkable ability to disguise his central interest in social ethics (perhaps even from himself) beneath the nonethical language of anthropology and psychology. Morton White has perhaps best characterized the puzzling personality of Veblen by referring to him as "the amoral moralist."

The moral ambiguity of Veblen's writings is also characteristic of many of the dissident thinkers discussed in this chapter, including Thurman Arnold. Generally, these were men of moral sensitivity who decried moralism, principled men who attacked universal principles. The meaning of their position is less ambiguous when considered primarily as a criticism of established systems of thought. The principles and moral inferences of these systems had drifted away from humanitarian values into a world of abstractions. Moreover, they had failed to take account of the "tumbling stream of events" which constitutes social change. The dissenters were revolting not against moral principle itself, but against socially uninformed principles which had ceased to be concerned with immediate human needs.

It is within this context of intellectual dissent, with its new methods of social study and its more or less avowed humanitarian impulse, that the philosophy of Thurman Arnold must be considered.

## NOTES

[1] Philip P. Wiener, *Evolution and the Founders of Pragmatism* (Cambridge: Harvard University Press, 1949), p. 20. Wiener, however, has documented the curious fact that none of the other club members except James ever used the term "pragmatism" in print until 1898. Holmes later did not recall the term used in club discussions despite Peirce's recollection that he mentioned it frequently on these occasions (pp. 21, 22). After subjecting Peirce's assertion to critical scrutiny, Wiener is still able to conclude that "Peirce brought together in his account of the genesis of pragmatism a historically important group of persons who . . . moved in the same intellectual atmosphere, and influenced each other in ways that shaped . . . ideas current in our thinking today" (pp. 25, 26).

[2] Ibid., p. 23  [3] p. 94.

[4] Ralph Barton Perry, *The Thought and Character of William James* (Boston: Little, Brown & Co., 1935), vol. 2, p. 408.

[5] Merle Curti, *The Social Ideas of American Educators* (Paterson, N.J.: Pageant Books, 1959), pp. 454–55.

[6] Wiener, *Evolution and the Founders of Pragmatism*, pp. 125–26. See also Curti, *Social Ideas of American Educators*, p. 457.

[7] Morton G. White, *The Origins of Dewey's Instrumentalism* (New York: Octagon Books, Inc., 1964), p. 4. In some colleges, Hall adds, faculty members were hired and fired by the founders as if they were day laborers. Other colleges were constantly falling under the control of state legislatures and ward politicians.

[8] Ibid., pp. 6–8, 32, 82, 95, 103–04.

[9] John Dewey, *Reconstruction in Philosophy* (Boston: Beacon Press, 1957), pp. 190–92. Original edition by Henry Holt & Co., 1920.

[10] Ibid., "Logical Method and Law," *Cornell Law Quarterly,* vol. 10 (December 1924), p. 27.

[11] Eric F. Goldman, *Rendezvous with Destiny* (New York: Vintage Books, 1956), pp. 122–23.

[12] Richard T. Ely, *Ground Under Our Feet* (New York: Macmillan, 1938), pp. 124–26.

[13] Ibid., pp. 132, 140. Although united against the sterility of orthodox economics, the members of the Saratoga group had some important differences among themselves. Simon Patten asserted that the principle of competition must give way to a more efficient, planned economy. John Bates Clark, on the other hand, continued to believe in the value of free competition and wished only to remedy its deficiencies. The ability of the group to agree on an unorthodox statement of principles despite individual differences was a notable achievement.

[14] Joseph Dorfman, *Thorstein Veblen and His America* (New York: Viking Press, 1934), pp. 18, 22.

[15] Ibid., p. 155 [16] p. 156.

[17] Thorstein Veblen, *The Theory of the Leisure Class* (New York: Modern Library, 1934). First published in 1899.

[18] Ibid., *The Theory of Business Enterprise* (New York: Charles Scribner's Sons, 1904).

[19] Joseph Dorfman's definitive biography is extremely valuable in understanding the origins of Veblen's "invidious distinction" between the disruptive businessman and the creative producer. Veblen was raised in a small Norwegian farming community during a period of rising agrarian bitterness toward business. Veblen was later to recall those days in bitter terms. The Scandinavian immigrants, by his account, settled as tillers of the soil while Americans from the East scattered over the same regions in the towns. The immigrants did the *work* of reclaiming the land while the native born in the towns carried on the *business* (described by Veblen as "prehensile" in nature, i.e., "directed to getting something for nothing at the expense of the immigrants). . . . The presumption in the mind of the honest businessmen was on the side of their own pecuniary advantage, leaving any doubts to be settled by litigation . . . brought by the foreign immigrants —who could be relied on to avoid all litigation under a system of law with which they had no acquaintance, before legal magistrates (businessmen) whom they had no reason to trust, in a language they could not understand." See Thorstein Veblen, *Imperial Germany and the Industrial Revolution* (New York: Viking Press, 1954), p. 335. Originally published in 1915. See also Dorfman, *Thorstein Veblen and His America,* p. 7.

[20] John M. Clark, "Recent Developments in Economics," *Recent Developments in the Social Sciences* (Philadelphia: Lippincott, 1927), p. 250.

[21] Joseph Dorfman, *The Economic Mind in American Civilization* (New York: Viking Press, 1949), vol. 3, p. 446.

[22] Allan G. Gruchy, *Modern Economic Thought—the American Contribution* (New York: Prentice-Hall, Inc., 1947). [23] Ibid., p. 11 [24] pp. 560–61.

[25] John R. Commons, *Legal Foundations of Capitalism* (New York: Macmillan, 1924).

[26] Kenneth H. Parsons, "Institutional Economics—Discussion," *American Economic Review—Papers and Proceedings,* vol. 47 (May 1957), pp. 22–23.

27 Gruchy, *Modern Economic Thought*, p. 240.   28 Ibid., pp. 568, 590.

29 Selig Perlman, "John Rogers Commons: 1862–1945," *Wisconsin Magazine of History*, vol. 29 (September 1945), pp. 25–27.

30 Kenneth E. Boulding, "A New Look at Institutionalism," *American Economic Review—Papers and Proceedings*, vol. 47 (May 1957), p. 7.

31 Forest G. Hill, "Wesley Mitchell's Theory of Planning," *Political Science Quarterly*, vol. 72 (1957), pp. 101–02.

32 Gruchy, *Modern Economic Thought*, pp. 395–96.

33 Dorfman, *The Economic Mind in American Civilization*, vol. 3, p. 402.

34 Charles H. Cooley, "Political Economy and Social Process," *Sociological Theory and Social Research* (New York: Henry Holt, 1930), p. 253. First published in 1918.

35 Walton H. Hamilton, "Charles Horton Cooley," *Social Forces*, vol. 8 (December 1929), p. 185.

36 Bernhard J. Stern, "The Ward–Ross Correspondence 1891–96," *American Sociologial Review*, vol. 3 (1938), p. 386.   37 Ibid., p. 391   38 p. 377.

39 Bernhard J. Stern, "Ward–Ross Correspondence III 1904–1905," *American Sociological Review*, vol. 13 (1948), p. 93.

40 Edward A. Ross, *Foundations of Sociology* (New York: Macmillan, 1905), pp. 10–12.   41 Ibid., p. 15   42 pp. 13–14.

43 See Jessie Bernard's review of Ross's autobiography in *American Sociological Review*, vol. 2 (April 1937), pp. 273–75. See also J. O. Hertzler, "Edward Alsworth Ross," *American Sociological Review*, vol. 16 (1951), p. 598.

44 See Edward A. Ross, *Social Control* (New York: Macmillan, 1929). Widely considered Ross's most impressive work as well as a solid contribution to the foundations of American sociological theory.

45 Ibid., *Seventy Years of It* (New York: D. Appleton Century Co., 1936), p. 180.

46 Ibid., *Sin and Society* (Boston and New York: Houghton Mifflin Co., 1907), p. 15.

47 Ibid., *Seventy Years of It*, p. 111. Ross's deep interest in developing attitudes hospitable to social reform is also evidenced by his authorship of a crisp, provocative high school text entitled *Civic Sociology* (New York: World Book Co., 1930). The author begins with a challenge: "Since the citizen will have to face such lively issues as personal liberty, commercialism, sectionalism, sectarianism, and class struggle, this book introduces the youth to them." Ross concludes with some general guidelines for young citizens including a call for alertness against highly organized special interests. "Unless many citizens are so shrewd that they recognize a special interest and . . . oppose it whenever it clashes with the general interest, we have a fight between a whale and a swordfish with the odds on the swordfish." p. 353.

48 William F. Ogburn, *On Culture and Social Change—Selected Papers*, edited by Otis D. Duncan (Chicago: University of Chicago Press, 1964). See Duncan's introduction, pp. viii–x.   49 Ibid., pp. 86, 90.

50 Ibid., p. 90. Despite the emphasis of his examples, Ogburn did not mean to preclude the possibility that cultural lag could be produced by a society's *nontechnical* features, e.g., literature, philosophy, or the arts, advancing beyond its *technical* development.

51 Quoted in Charles E. Merriam, *The Role of Politics in Social Change* (New York: New York University Press, 1936), p. 65.

52 Charles A. Beard, *An Economic Interpretation of the Constitution of the United States* (New York: Macmillan, 1935), p. 324. First published in 1913.

53 See Richard Hofstadter, *The Progressive Historians* (New York: Alfred A. Knopf, 1968), pp. 181–82.  54 Ibid., p. 185.

55 J. Allen Smith, *The Spirit of American Government* (New York: Macmillan, 1907).

56 See Hofstadter, *Progressive Historians,* pp. 192–93.

57 Ibid., pp. 196–97  58 p. 199.

59 Beard, *Economic Interpretation of the Constitution of the United States,* pp. 1, 15.  60 Ibid., p. 9.

61 Hofstadter, *Progressive Historians,* pp. 202–03.

62 Beard, *Economic Interpretation of the Constitution of the United States,* p. 1.  63 Ibid., p. 10  64 pp. 324–25.

65 See Hofstadter, *Progressive Historians,* pp. 230–37.

66 See Ellen D. Ellis, "Political Science at the Crossroads," *American Political Science Review,* vol. 21 (November 1927), pp. 773–76.

67 Arthur F. Bentley, *The Process of Government* (Bloomington, Ind.: Principia Press, Inc., 1935), p. 181. First published in 1908.

68 Ibid., p. 206  69 p. 205.

70 Charles E. Merriam, *Systematic Politics* (Chicago: University of Chicago Press, 1945), p. viii.

71 Leonard D. White (ed.), *The Future of Government in the United States: Essays in Honor of Charles E. Merriam* (Chicago: University of Chicago Press, 1942), p. vi.

72 Merriam, *Systematic Politics,* p. ix. Emphasis mine.

73 Ibid., *Role of Politics in Social Change,* p. 92.

74 White, *Future of Government in United States,* pp. vii, 14–15.

75 Merriam, *Role of Politics in Social Change,* p. 101.  76 Ibid., p. 132.

77 Oliver Wendell Holmes, Jr., *The Common Law* (Boston: Little, Brown & Co., 1923), p. 1. First published in 1881.

78 Ibid.  79 p. 35  80 ibid.

81 *Lochner* v. *New York.* 198 U.S. 45, 75 (1905).

82 Pound was then teaching and serving as Dean of the Law School at the University of Nebraska.

83 Paul Sayre, *The Life of Roscoe Pound* (Iowa City: State University of Iowa Press, 1948), p. 148.  84 Ibid., p. 149  85 p. 150.

86 Pound states that his adoption of "sociological jurisprudence" was mainly due to the influence of sociologists Edward A. Ross and Albion Small. See Roscoe Pound, "Sociology of Law," *Twentieth Century Sociology,* edited by Georges Gurvitch and W. E. Moore (New York: Philosophical Library, 1945), p. 335.

87 Ibid., p. 334.

88 Ibid., "Mechanical Jurisprudence," *Columbia Law Review,* vol. 8 (December 1908), pp. 609–10.

89 Karl N. Llewellyn, *Jurisprudence—Realism in Theory and Practice* (Chicago: University of Chicago Press, 1962), pp. 496–97. See also Wilfred Rumble, "Legal Realism, Sociological Jurisprudence and Mr. Justice Holmes," *Journal of the History of Ideas,* vol. 26, pp. 547–66.

90 As Rumble suggests (see note 89), Pound's dispute with the realists was probably related to a difference in political persuasion. Pound, a practicing Republican and a moderate reformer, was less eager to carry out a sociological

revolution in law than were the realists, many of whom were liberal Democrats inspired by early New Deal hopes for social reconstruction. Both disputants claimed Holmesian ancestry. Perhaps the hard-headed skepticism of Holmes (leading to his distinction between law and morals) was the father of legal realism while Pound's reformist sociological jurisprudence was its mother. The distinctive qualities of each parent were combined and exaggerated in such a way that neither spouse would be eager to claim the offspring.

[91] Fred V. Cahill, *Judicial Legislation* (New York: Ronald Press, 1952), p. 119.

[92] Harold G. Reuschlein, *Jurisprudence—Its American Prophets* (Indianapolis: Bobbs-Merrill Company, Inc., 1951), p. 233.   [93] Ibid., p. 208   [94] p. 288.

[95] Ely, *Ground Under Our Feet*, pp. 87–91.

[96] Dorfman, *Economic Mind in American Civilization*, vol. 3, p. 282.

[97] Ibid., p. 404.

[98] Ross, *Seventy Years of It*, pp. 116–19.

[99] Ibid., *Social Control*, p. 204.   [100] Ibid., pp. 213, 215–16.

[101] Gruchy, *Modern Economic Thought*, pp. 64–65.   [102] Ibid., pp. 75–76.

# CHAPTER II

# THE BACKGROUND, METHODS, AND VALUES OF ARNOLD

"No one," said Arnold in the preface to *Symbols of Government,* "escapes the constant necessity of dressing himself in a series of different uniforms or silk hats and watching himself go by." This is certainly a fitting theme for a man who played so many different roles in public and private life. His public career included service at the local, state, and national levels. At one time or another, he served in the legislative, executive, and judicial branches of government. Arnold's private career was no less diversified. He was a small town lawyer in Laramie, Wyoming, a senior partner in one of Washington's most successful law firms, Dean of the West Virginia Law School, and a professor of law at Yale. Arnold's social thought was characterized by methods and values accrued from these personal experiences.

Arnold was born in Laramie, Wyoming, in 1891, the son of Peter Arnold, a prosperous lawyer and rancher. Thurman's grandfather,

Franklin Arnold, had been a missionary in Africa and later became a Presbyterian pastor in Laramie. Arnold remembered him as a "kindly man" who, nevertheless, had a few "foibles peculiar to the Presbyterian faith of those times." On the Sabbath, which lasted from six o'clock Saturday evening until Monday morning, Franklin permitted no levity, games, or amusements. Thurman remembered his grandfather refusing to let him enter his pony in a race at the county fair. Franklin associated racing with gambling which went against his Presbyterian "foibles." The grandson was bitterly disappointed. "This incident," he recalled, "planted the seeds of skepticism about the old-time religion that have plagued and tormented me ever since." [1] Thurman Arnold was learning to call dogmas and creeds into question at an early age.

At the age of sixteen, he left Laramie to attend Princeton University where he encountered a dull and irrelevant approach to education. "Ancient texts were studied as if they existed in a vacuum, wholly apart from the culture of the civilizations that created them." [2] The Princeton student of Arnold's day was not given a broad understanding of social and political processes, but was sent on a quest for abstract truth. As Arnold recalls: "We read extracts from the philosophers from Plato to William James, though we read them not as part of the thinking or the values of the time in which they wrote but as seekers for abstract truth which had no relation to time or place." [3]

Hegel and Spinoza were considered "top drawer truth seekers" while the pragmatism of William James was considered suspect "because it seemed to deny fundamental truths." [4] Princeton in the 1960s, commented Arnold, is entirely different from the Princeton of his student days: "Just as the old Princeton reflected an age of certainties and conventions, so the new Princeton and other educational institutions reflect an age of questioning and discovery." [5]

Arnold somehow managed to master the abstract formulas of the Princeton curriculum and graduated in four years with Phi Beta Kappa honors. He entered the Harvard Law School in the fall of 1911. Although Harvard professors "seemed intellectual giants" when compared with the Princeton faculty, "the world of the Harvard Law School was as much a world of eternal verities and absolute certainties as it had been at Princeton." [6] Law and economics were considered the principal fields. Dabblers in sociology or psychology were suspect. Legal training stressed the "narrow logic of the law, the building of legal principle on the solid basis of a long line of precedents, and the analysis of cases in class by the Socratic method." [7]

After graduating from Harvard Law School in 1914, Arnold practiced law in Chicago until 1917 when the United States declared war against Germany. During the war, Arnold served in Europe as an artillery officer. He remembered his life at the front as an exciting but uncomfortable experience and that he was mercifully spared the worst horrors of war: "There was the noise of shells exploding and gas attacks too frequent to recite in detail here. But the artillery was far enough behind the front lines for our casualties to be relatively light. The chief discomforts were the cold and the wet, which I will never forget." [8]

After the war, Arnold returned to Laramie to practice law and to dabble successfully in local politics. In 1920, he was elected to the Wyoming House of Representatives, distinguishing himself as the only Democrat to survive the Harding landslide of that year. Quick to perceive the humor in his situation, Arnold announced to the assembled legislature which was in the process of electing a Speaker: "Mr. Speaker, the Democratic party caucused last night, and when the name of Thurman Arnold was mentioned, it threw its hat up in the air and cheered for fifteen minutes. I therefore wish to put his name in nomination for Speaker of this House." [9] Noting that the Speaker was confused at this unexpected departure from his carefully prepared agenda, Arnold rose again and said, "Mr. Speaker, some irresponsible Democrat has put my name in nomination and I wish to withdraw it." [10] The ability to perceive and deftly exploit the comical aspects of a situation was later to become a hallmark of Arnold's social and political writing.

When his legislative term ended, he ran for mayor of Laramie and was elected by a narrow margin. Unlike the philosophical Arnold of later years, he was something of a crusading politician. "At the time I ran," he said, "for reasons obscure to me at the present time, I was an ardent Prohibitionist." [11] As mayor, he annoyed many of Laramie's good citizens by actually enforcing the prohibition laws.[12]

The years in Laramie, practicing law and dabbling in local politics, were happy ones for Thurman Arnold. He participated in, and enjoyed, many of the middle-class activities that Sinclair Lewis so deftly debunked in his portrayal of George Babbitt. Arnold sang inspirational songs at Lion's Club lunches, was a vestryman of his church, a leader in Elks Club festivals, a member of the Chamber of Commerce, and a speaker on each Memorial Day.[13] His decision to leave Laramie in 1927 was made with deep regret. On the day before his departure, Arnold lunched with his wife, mother, and father at the downtown hotel, and from the next room Arnold's fellow Lions burst forth with "For He's a Jolly Good Fellow." His wife was so moved that she began weeping on the bosom of the hotel waitress. When the Arnolds finally departed, fifty cars escorted them to the Divide of the Rockies.[14]

The happy years in Laramie were not unrelated to Arnold's later vigorous attempts to enforce the antitrust laws. During the 1920s, he contended, the antitrust laws were ignored. Giant corporations, mostly in the East, absorbed local industries in the West and the South. Because the decline of locally based industry meant the decline of locally based law practices, Arnold concluded in 1927 that there was no future in Laramie for the local lawyer.[15] He had learned from personal experience that unchecked economic concentration destroys widespread economic opportunity.

Fortunately, a new professional opportunity was made possible by Dean Roscoe Pound of the Harvard Law School, who remembered Arnold as an original scholar. On Pound's recommendation, Arnold was offered the deanship of the law school at West Virginia University.[16] Arnold gratefully accepted the offer, and by so doing, launched himself into what was to become a prominent academic career. During his deanship at West Virginia, Arnold developed a habit of prodigious writing. He authored nineteen book reviews and articles in the *West Virginia Law Quarterly* over a period of three years. In 1930, Arnold accepted an appointment to the law faculty of Yale. "The years that followed," he recalled, "were among the most interesting and exciting of my life." [17] Dean Charles E. Clark had assembled a formidable faculty including William O. Douglas, Walton Hale Hamilton, Arthur Corbin, Wesley Sturges, and Underhill Moore. The general attitude of the faculty was against dogma of all kinds.[18]

During the 1930s, the Yale law faculty was busy eliminating old courses and introducing new ones thought to be better adapted to the realities of judicial institutions. The new emphasis was centered not on legal theory but on the actual operations of business and legal institutions.[19] Specialists from other disciplines, including economist Walton Hamilton and psychologist Edward S. Robinson, were employed to provide a broader perspective for the study of these institutions. Arnold's first book, *The Symbols of Government,* grew out of a seminar given by him and Professor Robinson on the psychological foundations of the law. As a professor, Arnold approached the law from a variety of non-legal perspectives. Some students found his broad-ranging lectures difficult to follow: "He frequently started on a set topic, wandered off into the mythical aspects of economics, progressed to the mores of politics, and so on until lost at last, he brought himself up short with a genial, 'Now what the hell am I supposed to be talking about?' " [20] Arnold fitted well into the intellectual environment of the Yale Law School with its sharp distinction between the ideals and the actual operations of institutions, its broad interdisciplinary approach to the law, and its general distrust of all dogmatisms.

During the summer of 1933, Arnold had his first experience in government service. His assignment was to assist Jerome Frank, then general counsel of the Agricultural Adjustment Administration, on problems concerning the constitutionality of the new Agricultural Adjustment Act. The Department of Agriculture was "in a perfect bedlam" when Arnold arrived. "Everything that was being done was unconventional and unheard of, and, therefore, unconstitutional." [21] The task of the legal section was to demonstrate that the new governmental programs aimed at relieving distress did not violate "the sanctity of such magic phrases as 'proper delegation of powers' . . . and 'due process of law.' " [22] Certainly Arnold's brief experience with the Department of Agriculture strengthened his conviction, expressed later in *The Folklore of Capitalism,* that practical humanitarian measures, to be accepted, must be draped in the prevailing economic and legal symbols of the day. His job, in the summer of 1933, was to find an acceptable constitutional symbolism to accompany unconventional public efforts to relieve economic distress.

Arnold's next summer vacation was spent as a legal advisor to Frank Murphy, then governor general of the Philippines, assisting him in the administration of the Sugar Control Act. From 1935, until his sabbatical leave from Yale in 1937, Arnold spent his summer vacations in Washington as a trial examiner for the Securities and Exchange Commission chaired by William O. Douglas, who was then investigating corporate reorganizations.[23] This experience provided the basis for Arnold's brilliant and witty chapter on corporate reorganizations which appeared later in *The Folklore of Capitalism.*

During his sabbatical leave from Yale, Arnold served as assistant to Robert Jackson, who was then head of the Tax Division of the Department of Justice.[24] He used his spare time to complete *Folklore,* which became a best seller and is probably his most important contribution to American political and social thought. Soon after the publication of *Folklore,* Arnold was appointed assistant attorney general in charge of the Antitrust Division of the Justice Department. Yale University, after having granted its absentee professor a two-year leave following his sabbatical and finding him still engrossed in antitrust work, announced that he had resigned.[25] Arnold reluctantly accepted the fact that he could not carry on his antitrust work and have his academic tenure too.

His term as chief trustbuster lasted from March 1938 to March 1943. There was a great deal of early skepticism about Arnold's attitude toward the antitrust laws among those who had read *Folklore.* The author had stated in that book that the antitrust laws were little more than a ceremony to celebrate the ideal of rugged individualism, and that they had actually been a barrier to effective regulation of large corporations. "I wondered," Arnold reminisced, "just how . . . I was going to explain my present enthusiasm for the antitrust laws in the light of what I had written just a year before." [26] His answer, he decided, was that in writing the book he was merely observing the faulty operation of the antitrust laws during the 1920s. Once in office, he would try to improve the situation.

Any doubts about the sincerity of Arnold's avowed intention to enforce the antitrust laws were dispelled soon after he took office. By the end of his five-year term, Arnold had instituted 44 percent of all antitrust suits which had been brought by the Justice Department since the passage of the Sherman Act in 1890. Appropriations for the Antitrust Division were about $473,000 in the fiscal year 1938. Five years later, they had risen to $1.8 million. Over the same period, the Division's personnel increased from 111 to 496.[27] Perhaps Arnold's most important contribution was the revival of the antitrust laws as a basis for public policy. As one student of Arnold's trust-busting career has observed: "When he took office it was common, and when he left office rare, to encounter the view that the policy of the antitrust laws was out of date, that offenses under the laws were merely technical, and that the protection of the public interest must be sought exclusively in government regulation of business and in the public spirit shown by business men." [28]

After five stormy years in the Antitrust Division, Arnold found himself attracted to a much more peaceful and serene career. In March 1943, President Roosevelt appointed him judge of the United States Court of Appeals for the District of Columbia. ". . . when I accepted the judgeship," Arnold recalled, "I confidently expected to spend the rest of my life in a position of great dignity, with long vacations in the summer, in an atmosphere where the wicked cease from troubling and the weary are at rest." [29]

In spite of his hopeful expectations, Arnold soon discovered that he was not temperamentally suited to what he had earlier described as the "priestly function" of the judge. His preference for partisan argument rather than for impartial decision made him doubt whether he could ever be "an ornament to the bench." The role of a judge was simply too restricted for a vigorous advocate like Thurman Arnold: "I was impatient with legal precedents that seemed to me to reach an unjust result. I felt restricted by the fact that a judge has no business writing or speaking on controversial subjects. A judge can talk about human liberties, the rule of law above men, and similar abstractions. All of them seemed to me dull subjects." [30]

For these reasons, Arnold resigned from the bench in the spring of 1945 to resume the private practice of law. There was no bitterness toward judicial institutions in this decision. In his earlier book, *The Symbols of Government*, Arnold had pointed out the social necessity of judicial symbols such as the impersonal rule of law above men. A judge, to play a moving part in the judicial ceremony, must believe in its symbols. Judge Arnold's discovery that he was temperamentally unsuited for this role did not lead him to debunk the role itself or the robed figures who gave it life.

Arnold's first law partner after he resigned from the Court of Appeals was Arne C. Wiprud, a former associate in the Department of Justice.[31] Wiprud was an expert in transportation, and returned to government service when the new firm's expectation of transportation business did not materialize. Arnold then asked Abe Fortas, who was planning to resign as Under Secretary of the Interior, to enter into a law partnership. The firm of Arnold and Fortas was launched in January

1946. Arnold considered this "the smartest decision I ever made." [32] One of the original associates in the new firm was Walton Hale Hamilton, the brilliant institutional economist and former professor at the Yale Law School.

Arnold and Fortas had been in practice together for less than two years when they asked Paul Porter, who had just returned from ambassadorial duties in Greece, to join them as a third partner. Arnold, Fortas and Porter proved to be a viable combination, and the three men remained together until August 1965 when Abe Fortas was appointed by President Johnson to the United States Supreme Court.

One of the characteristics which came to distinguish the firm of Arnold, Fortas and Porter was its courageous involvement in civil liberties issues. Soon after Porter joined the firm, seven State Department employees who had been summarily dismissed from their jobs on loyalty grounds came to the office seeking legal counsel. Their stories convinced the partners that, unlike other summary dismissals in time of stress, dismissals carrying the stigma of disloyalty must not take place without a fair trial complete with sworn testimony, cross-examination of witnesses, and other evidence acceptable in court. The firm's attorneys, with the aid of publicity given to the case by the New York *Herald Tribune,* managed to persuade the State Department to remove the "disloyalty" notations from the records of the ousted employees.[33]

The firm's practice of giving free legal aid to innocent employees dismissed on loyalty grounds soon brought a flood of requests for help. To relieve the pressure, the attorneys sought a test case through which they hoped to settle the broad issues that were at stake. They chose the case of Dorothy Bailey who had been dismissed from the United States Employment Service on the ground that an informant claimed to have seen her at a Communist meeting. The Loyalty Board which upheld the charge refused to disclose the identity of her accusers or even the time and place of her alleged disloyal acts.[34]

To the bitter disappointment of Arnold, Fortas and Porter, the District of Columbia Court of Appeals held that Miss Bailey's dismissal raised no constitutional issues and that judicial intervention was therefore unwarranted. The partners appealed the case to the Supreme Court which split 4-4 on the issue, leaving the lower court decision unimpaired. After the Bailey case, Arnold, Fortas and Porter concluded that they had carried the legal struggle as far as possible under present court rulings, and sharply reduced their "loyalty practice." [35]

The firm, even after the disappointment of the Bailey decisions, continued to take exceptional cases. The most publicized of these was the case of Owen Lattimore, a professor of Johns Hopkins University, who was accused by Senator McCarthy of being a Communist. The firm provided counsel for Lattimore throughout the hearings before a Senate subcommittee chaired by Senator Pat McCarran. Arnold described these hearings as a psychological ordeal designed to trap the witness rather than a fair procedure to obtain the truth from him.[36] After the hearings, the Justice Department charged that Lattimore had perjured himself when he testified that he had never been a "promoter of Communist interests." [37] As Arnold pointed out, the meaning given this phrase by the government was broad enough to include anyone who favored aid to Russia during the Second World War or aid to Tito's Yugoslavia. After a bitter struggle, Arnold, Fortas and Porter were able to get a dismissal of the charges against Lattimore in the courts.

The economic risks taken by the firm in defending Lattimore and others suspected of disloyalty did not materialize. Arnold, Fortas and Porter remained one of Washington's most successful law firms. Its clients have included such large and prestigious corporations as the Coca Cola Company, Pan American Airways, Lever Brothers, Western Union Telegraph, the Sun Oil Company, and the American Broadcasting Company.[38]

Arnold continued to be actively engaged in his private law practice until his death in November 1969. During the last years of his life he was a strong supporter of the Johnson Administration. In 1967 he gave public support to the President's increasingly unpopular Vietnam policies by joining the Citizen's Committee for Peace with Freedom in Vietnam, along with other prominent figures such as Dean Acheson, Paul Douglas, Omar Bradley, and Harry Truman.

The following year Arnold crossed political swords with Senator Sam Ervin (D., N.C.) in a debate published by the *Washington Post* (September 15, 1968) on the "Pros and Cons of the Abe Fortas Nomination." Ervin charged that Fortas lacked the judicial "self-restraint" necessary for a Chief Justice of the United States Supreme Court. Arnold replied in behalf of his long-time friend and law partner: "As for

Justice Fortas's personal capacity for restraint, that was demonstrated beyond cavil during the recent hearings by the calm patience with which he withstood the widely condemned abuse visited upon him by one senatorial inquisitor" [Senator Strom Thurmond (R., S.C.)]. Arnold continued to support Fortas even after the damaging charges of financial impropriety were brought against him. The Fortas controversy was the last of many "fair fights and foul" in the varied career of Thurman Arnold. His contribution to American social thought has certainly been enhanced by a background as diverse as the life experiences of five interesting and successful men.

Thurman Arnold's methods of social study have much in common with the methods of the dissenting intellectuals of late nineteenth- and early twentieth-century America. These methods, discussed in Chapter I, were characterized by philosophical relativism, detached perspective, historicism, holism, interest in philosophical lag and ideology, and conclusions couched in terms of social criticism and reform.

Arnold's philosophical relativism is found in his attack on the notion of absolute, universal, and unchanging ideals. "The world," he contended "will never see a permanently valid philosophy until science discovers a method of making Time stand still." [39] Changes in fundamental values are, to Arnold, a function of life; these values come not from above but from human organizations "which can no more help producing principles than a hen can keep from laying eggs." [40]

Because principles are relative to organizations, they should serve organizations, not cripple them. When organizations are forced to conform to principles that are deemed to be universal and unchanging, they can no longer carry on practical humanitarian activities. Arnold observed that in the Middle Ages the Church was not judged by its effectiveness as an organization, but by whether its creeds conformed with standards of universal truth. The missionary activities of most modern churches show a complete change of attitude. Medical attention to underprivileged groups is now thought to be more important than creedal services. [41]

Unlike the missionary activities of the churches, the practical humanitarian activities of modern government are crippled by the strictures of universal principles. The new economic measures of the 1930s, observed Arnold, were heartily condemned before they were even tried because they were said to violate unchanging legal and economic principles. Where these principles are not threatened, the government can take steps to alleviate human problems with dispatch and confidence. The attempted rescue of the American heroine, Amelia Earhart, provided Arnold with an example. Here there was no conflict with spiritual principles because "the doubts about spending every available national resource in the rescue . . . were confined to a very few people." [42] In an amusing passage, Arnold imagined how difficult it might have been to initiate the rescue operation had the defenders of universal economic principles deemed it unsound: "Everyone would have agreed that people in distress must be rescued. They would have insisted, however, that the problem was intimately tied up with balancing the national budget, improving the character of people lost at sea, stopping the foolhardy from adventuring and at the same time encouraging the great spirit of adventure and so on *ad infinitum.*" [43]

When universal economic principles are threatened, government finds itself powerless to take practical action. Arnold illustrated his point by reference to a shanty colony in New York City which was being removed to make way for a new building. The newspaper reports of impoverished people leaving their makeshift dwellings evoked sympathy, but nothing could be done about it. To give them a dole would have a tendency to undermine the principle of rugged individualism. After the demolition work began, two unconscious men were found under one of the dwellings. As if by magic, Arnold said, principles were forgotten and "pure benevolence took charge." The most expensive medical equipment was employed without delay. The objective was to get the men to the hospital, not to discuss abstract philosophy. [44]

Arnold believed that adherence to universal principles has always been the chief obstacle to social experimentation and discovery. To those who fear social experiments, he replied: ". . . the human race has caused itself more suffering because of its theories than by all the experiments ever conducted. Revolutions are not carried on by experimentalists, but by people who believe in theories with a fanaticism which allows them cheerfully to kill anyone who disagrees with even the details of their abstract formulae." [45] According to Arnold, there are no absolute or universal principles. Principles grow out of and must serve organizations. When accepted and followed literally, universal ideals tend to impose unnecessary sacrifices on human beings by crippling practical organizations.

Arnold's philosophical relativism was reinforced by his historical perspective. It is primarily from history that Arnold learned to doubt the literal truth of today's universal principles. He pointed out that ideals thought to be universal truths in past historical epochs are today widely recognized as folklore or superstition. Some of Arnold's most brilliant and amusing passages describe the similarities between yesterday's folklore and today's universal principles. His discourse on the introduction of quinine as a medicinal agent is a good example of his witty and revealing use of history.

When the Jesuits discovered quinine in 1638, its use as a drug was viewed as an alarming departure from established healing methods such as the bleeding process. Since quinine did not relieve the "noxious vapors" in the blood, it was only an "artificial panacea" despite the patient's delusion that he felt better. The leading thinkers of the day were convinced that the relief of a few sufferers could never be worth the overthrow of all the medical principles of the past.[46] Moreover, the Jesuits were regarded as "the most dangerous religious bureaucrats of the time. . . ." Their remedies could not be adopted without adopting their pernicious religious principles. "And so," Arnold concluded, "the dreaded spector of Jesuitism hung over the use of quinine, as Communism and Fascism hang over soil conservation and crop insurance today." [47]

How then, did quinine ever come to be accepted? "Fortunately," said Arnold, "the unlearned people of the time, like those of today, were constantly forgetting the great moral issues of the future for the practical comfort of the moment." Even so, quinine "had to be introduced by a quack who concealed it in a curious compound of irrelevant substances." [48]

Arnold's discourse on quinine throws both satire and historical perspective simultaneously on the philosophical opposition to the New Deal relief measures. It also demonstrates Arnold's conviction that controversial social and economic measures must be dressed up in irrelevant economic and legal symbols to gain public acceptance.

Two additional examples illustrate Arnold's skillful use of historical satire against the august legal and economic philosophers opposing the New Deal. He pointed out that during the Middle Ages, the learned scholars of the University of Paris occupied an authoritative position in medicine similar to the position of the United States Supreme Court in government. The attitudes of these medieval scholars, he noted, were similar in many ways to those of the Supreme Court justices:

> They spent their lives studying those fundamental principles, the violation of which brings ruin. Their logic was as unassailable as the economic and legal logic of today. They had the same distrust of immediate practical advantage, and the same fear of . . . impending moral disaster lying in wait to destroy the national character of a people who deserted fundamental principles to gain present ends.[49]

Arnold satirized the conservative economists of the New Deal period in a similar fashion by comparing them to the Roman augurs who "studied the flight of birds and examined the entrails of geese." When the Roman proconsuls proposed objectionable legislation, the augurs would make their studies and discover bad omens for the future.[50]

Arnold's philosophical relativism, reinforced by historical perspective, was closely related to his dislike of elaborate logical systems built on universal principles and formal definitions. He disputed the notion that careful definition produces clarity in thinking. "It is not generally recognized," he argued, "that the more we define our terms the less descriptive they become and the more difficulty we have in using them."[51] Arnold asserted that the analyst of social institutions should never try to define anything, and that he should attempt instead "to choose words and illustrations which will arouse the proper mental associations with his readers." Max Lerner, in reviewing *The Folklore of Capitalism,* noted Arnold's preference for exposition by illustration. "The book," he commented, "grows not by a series of syllogisms, but by an aggregation of examples."[52] Arnold believed that attempts at formal definition not only make description difficult, but create a set of abstractions which become values in themselves: "The actual result of dialectic definitions of social values is only to create a group of words like fascism, communism, regimentation, bureaucracy, etc., which impede practical methods of distributing goods."[53]

The purpose of logical definition, concluded Arnold, is not clear exposition but the resolution of contradictory ideals within vague abstractions. "The law," he observed, "which is above all a method of reconciling conflicting ideals, becomes so heavy with definitions that it is almost unintelligible."[54] Arnold's distrust of formal definitions and formal logic led him to concentrate on a "series of observations" rather than the formulation of an integrated, logically consistent philosophical system.

Although Arnold gave no precise definitions for his central concepts, his gift of clear rhetoric rescued them from obscurity. *Institutions* are described as human organizations which give prestige, morale, and purpose to their members. Institutions may be engaged in "practical" functions like the production and distribution of goods, or in "ceremonial" functions which honor the cherished ideals of society, or in both simultaneously. *Ideals* and *Folklore* are used interchangeably; they are principles believed to be objectively true, but in actuality are ideological supports for the prestige and morale of institutions. *Symbols* are given a broader connotation including both "ideals" (or "folklore") and the many ceremonies by which society dramatizes these ideals.

Another important characteristic of Arnold's approach to social studies was his refusal to be bound by the traditional boundaries of a single academic discipline. He believed that social phenomena cannot be understood unless all their interrelated aspects are considered together. Thus, Arnold described "political dynamics" as: "A science *about* society which treats its ideals, its literature, its principles of religion, law, economics, political systems, creeds and mythologies as part of a single whole and not as separate subjects, each with its own independent universe of principles." [55] He quoted approvingly from Charles H. Cooley's *Social Process* wherein the late professor of sociology asserted: "In social inquiries we are not dealing, usually, with distinct and measurable forces but with a complex of forces *no one of which can be understood and measured apart from the rest.*" [56]

Arnold was of the opinion that the rigid separation of insulated disciplines prevents the study of institutions as they actually operate. Thus, schools of economics blithely ignore political implications. Arnold cited as an example an economist who opposed the gold purchase plan of the New Deal period. When asked if he had considered the effect of the plan on the farm strike, he replied that this was a political consideration outside the realm of economic judgment.[57]

Arnold demonstrated that the artificial separation of economics, law, and sociology enables these disciplines to base their principles on contradictory conceptions of human nature. Economic man is an "automatic fellow" who operates on the principle of intelligent selfishness. He does not need to be preached to because his sins automatically cancel each other. This is all assured by economic laws which he cannot help following.[58] Legal man, on the other hand, needs "to be preached to in order to save him from sin. He is capable of being trained by judicial parables and statutory exhortation." [59] Arnold explained that economic man usually operates in larger affairs, while legal man is confined to minor ones. Thus, economic man justifies the failure of the law to deal with matters of broad economic scope.[60]

Selfish economic man and moral legal man, however, left practical humanitarian values unrepresented in the academic world. To fill this gap a new discipline called sociology was created, and the sociologist "represented a sort of humanitarian man, intent to discover ways and means for the alleviation of human misery." [61] The creation of sociology was a benefit to all concerned because the philanthropists now had a separate logical domain of their own and "would not interfere too much with legal or economic ways of thinking." [62]

Arnold's broad holistic approach to social studies went beyond criticism of isolated, self-contained disciplines. Polite chatting across established disciplinary lines is not what Arnold meant by broad-ranging social analysis. "Broad points of view," he believed, "are not congenial to the attitude which has departmentalized our institutions of learning." The academic world has been divided into "little irregular patches of domain." The separate groups occupying these scholarly dominions "have spent endless effort building books and articles on these properties" and will not have them "taken away without due process." For this reason, talking across established boundaries is tolerated by academicians while crossing over them is not: "It is all right for the neighbors to get together now and then for a housewarming or for a cooperative effort. . . . But when one man crosses to his neighbors domain . . . as if he contemplated changing the boundaries, he is greeted with suspicion and alarm." [63]

It is probably more accurate to describe Arnold's broad-ranging approach to social studies as "transdisciplinary" rather than "interdisciplinary." Instead of talking across boundaries, he believed in making the boundaries themselves less distinct. Specialists are needed to view the social whole from a certain perspective. However, when scholars attempt to detach a part from this whole and study it in isolation, distortion results. The pooling of resources by specialists from such isolated disciplines is likely to produce "cross sterilization."

Arnold combined a broad holistic approach to social studies with the perspective of an anthropologist. This perspective is characterized by detachment from the prevailing norms of the society under consideration. The first obstacle which confronts the anthropological observer is the artificial separation of learned disciplines which prevents the study of institutions as they actually operate. Arnold realized, however, that the fragmentation of the academic world has deep psychological roots and will not yield to any simple reorganization plan. It is precisely because insulated disciplines do not describe the actual operations of institutions that they can continue to provide rational proofs of the prevailing legal and economic faiths. "Therefore," concluded Arnold, "he who seeks to unite the legal and the social sciences fails to recognize that the climate of opinion which created them compels them to be kept apart." [64] Conventional approaches to law and economics must, therefore, remain unchanged until the climate of opinion changes.

Rather than destroying traditional approaches, Arnold recommended the introduction of a new approach which he hoped the academic community would learn to tolerate along with the old ones. He called this a "science *about* society" which is distinguished by its detachment from prevailing mores and its study of society as "a single whole." During his teaching years at Yale, Arnold participated in introducing this new approach into the law school curriculum. He believed that the inspirational study *of* law could coexist with the anthropological study *about* law.

Arnold contended that academicians, being mainly concerned with inspirational philosophies of what society ought to be, leave to the politicians the task of dealing with society as it is: "It is, I think, this habit of the philosophical mind of first determining what they want to look for, before they actually look, which makes them inept in actual organization." [65] This is the reason, Arnold concluded, that "we always find politicians . . . running the actual day-to-day government while the intellectuals are writing its songs and poetry." [66]

Arnold's main interest was in the detached study of the ideals or folklore of contemporary society. From such a study, one comes to recognize that "these ideals may have little to do with conduct and yet much to do with acceptance and power." The dissector of ideals learns "what to expect of these values . . . in action" and to predict "the verbal expression of any reform which gives it the best chance of public acceptance." [67]

54

The anthropological study of social folklore, in Arnold's view, can loosen the stranglehold of universal principles over practical organizations. By understanding the social impact of ideals, organizers can manipulate them to gain acceptance for practical humanitarian measures. Although Arnold confined philosophers to the cheerleading section of society, he maintained that they are nevertheless essential. Society cannot live on practical organization alone; it will always need its philosophical bards to provide the inspiration and the mystery that all men, including the practical organizers, need.

Like Thorstein Veblen, Arnold used the anthropological approach as a subtle method of social criticism. Max Lerner has observed that the writings of Arnold and Veblen are characterized by "corrosive detachment" rather than overt social protest or utopian schemes. Arnold's *Folklore of Capitalism,* he concludes, "belongs in the category of corrosive books, which eat away the past complacencies without the removal of which future constructions are impossible." [68] The spirit and style of Arnold's social criticism are perhaps best captured in one of his own terse comments. "Nothing disturbs the attitude of religious worship," he said, "so much as a few practical observations." [69]

Yet Arnold considered his primary purpose to be constructive rather than corrosive. His objective was to fashion social reform out of a context of irrational folklore, for he believed more firmly in the inevitable irrationality of politics than did most of the dissenting American intellectuals of the late nineteenth and early twentieth centuries. John Dewey, John R. Commons, Wesley Mitchell, and Charles Merriam, for example, were as acutely aware of the important role of irrational symbols in politics as was Arnold. However, their primary concern was to lay a reliable empirical foundation for more rational and scientific politics. Arnold, on the other hand, concentrated on the political manipulation of irrational symbols for the purpose of social reform. This aspect of Arnold's thought has been noted by Max Lerner who distinguishes him from other members of the school of "legal realism." The realist, he points out, believes there is something more "real" than the symbols of the law and goes off in pursuit of that something. Arnold, on the other hand, became fascinated with the symbols themselves. "For he sees that the ritual holds a subjective sway over men's minds, largely because of its correspondence with their desire for the dramatic and the symbolic." [70]

Arnold's emphasis on the expedient use of irrational symbols and

*55*

ceremonies also distinguished him from Thorstein Veblen who, in many ways, can be considered his intellectual predecessor. Veblen's ideal was the rational productive engineer, while his scorn was reserved for the ceremonial and ritualistic aspects of society. Arnold shared Veblen's admiration for the productive technician, but, as one observer has noted, he also believed ". . . that irrationality often serves social purposes, that men live by ideals and dreams, and not logic, and that the ceremonies of law and business are often necessary if the institutions of law and business are to retain men's allegiances." [71]

Arnold's advice to the social reformer was not to make politics more rational, but to learn to use irrational symbols for practical purposes. "When institutions fail to function," he asserted, "reforms must be attempted with something like the same point of view with which a trained psychiatrist reforms an individual." [72] Such a point of view recognizes the importance of irrational impulses in human behavior and attempts to direct those impulses into constructive channels. The psychiatric viewpoint, applied to society, "recognizes that drama and ceremony are as important as food and shelter and overemphasizes neither." [73]

Arnold shocked many of the readers of his *Symbols of Government* by boldly suggesting that the art of government was similar to running an insane asylum wherein the opinions and beliefs of the inmates are not taken literally but treated clinically.[74] Arnold was suggesting, in other words, that the attitudes of the public be psychologically manipulated by scientific methods to make people more comfortable. The political scientist, he asserted, "may try to learn how to harness the emotional reactions of people to words, and make them a tremendous source of motive power." [75]

Arnold's writings during the 1930s strongly urged politicians to make expediency, not principles, their guide to action: "The idea that there are principles above political expediency and that political expediency can never be a principle, [sic] is common to nearly all governmental philosophy except that of Machiavelli." [76] This idea, Arnold concluded, "lies beneath our fear of taking any unprecedented action in an emergency." Moreover, it stops experimentation, "which is man's greatest road to discovery." [77]

There is an apparent moral ambiguity in Arnold's writings during the 1930s, for, while counseling political expediency, he was also clearly committed to humanitarian principles. In evaluating rising organizations, he contended that the observer needs only to worry about "the character of the people who are gradually coming into power. Does he think that they are good organizers and at the same time tolerant and humanitarian?" [78]

Arnold's humanitarianism was also manifest in his 1935 prediction of the social creed of the future. He admitted that in making such speculations he had "deserted the objective position . . . and become a preacher and an advocate, rather than an anthropologist." [79] The fundamental creed of the past was that man works only for his personal profit. This basic tendency, while its excesses must be curbed by society, was considered part of nature's great plan. The new creed, said Arnold, will state that man works only for his fellowman, and *this* tendency, when properly curbed, is the great plan of society.[80] Arnold did not regard the humanitarian creed as any more true or false than the vital, morale-building creeds of the past, e.g., that man works only for the love of pure women, a future life, or personal profit.[81] Arnold's speculations on the social creed of the future seemed to represent a value preference. Under the old economic creed, he observed, there was incidental acknowledgment of the humanitarian, but the place of honor was given to the man who worked for personal gain. Under the new creed, these roles are reversed,[82] leaving the very strong impression that Arnold preferred an ethical creed and a social system which puts the humanitarian in society's driver's seat and the moneymaker in the rumble seat.

Arnold did not attempt to enshrine his humanitarian values in formal definition, but he did give them a simple operational meaning in terms of maximum production and distribution of goods in society. Institutions, he said, "are to be judged by their utility in the distribution of physical comforts and in the development of an attitude of spiritual peace." [83] The last phrase constituted, for Arnold, a second value which puts certain limitations on humanitarianism itself. "Spiritual peace" is related to tolerance. When a society marches single-mindedly to the tune of one creed, spiritual peace and social stability are lost in suppression: "Fanatical devotion to this single (humanitarian) ideal is such that it makes human liberty an unimportant value, and even kindness is stifled for purely humanitarian motives. There are explosive dangers to world peace and security in such fanaticism." [84]

The apparent moral ambiguity created by Arnold's commitment to political expediency above principle, and to humanitarian principle at the same time, becomes less puzzling when viewed in the context of the Depression. Prevailing principles and ideals during the 1930s had become intolerably at odds with humanitarian considerations. In 1930, for example, President Hoover approved a Congressional appropriation to save the livestock of stricken Arkansas farmers, but he opposed an additional appropriation to feed the farmers and their families. Relief money from the government, he noted, "would have injured the spiritual responses of the American people . . . we are dealing with the intangibles of . . . ideals." [85] President Hoover's statement suggests that, during the early 1930s, acts of political expediency were the only way to break the crust of traditional moral principles and to make way for humanitarian action.

The ideological spirit of the times largely explains how Arnold came to view moral principles as anathema to humanitarian benevolence. The word "humanitarian" is associated in his early writings with the word "practical" and with expedient action. Arnold's rejection of ideals as guides for political action represented his reaction to the growing disparity between respectable legal and economic ideals on the one hand and humanitarian ideals on the other. Like many dissident intellectuals during the late nineteenth and early twentieth centuries, Arnold was revolting, not against moral principle itself, but against socially uninformed principles that had become indifferent to human needs. As one observer has noted, "Like most great debunkers, he [Arnold] seemed to attack all morality, but he was really only concerned to destroy any morality that thought people should starve on principle." [86]

In later years, when Arnold observed the skillful use of psychological manipulation for pecuniary purposes on the one hand and the growth of moral principles with humanitarian purposes on the other, he came to trust expediency less and principles more. Max Lerner anticipated the first of these developments by observing in 1938 that Arnold's opportunistic emphasis on effective techniques "if torn out of the context of Arnold's own pattern, could be fitted into a pattern that would begin to look sinister." [87]

Eighteen years later, in 1956, Arnold commented that "the new conception of governing people by the manipulation of symbols and attitudes" had not brought pleasant results. It had brought the psychological manipulations of modern advertising in place of the financial manipulations of Wall Street. It had, moreover, "led to the belief of the Communist that he may manipulate men's minds with conscious hypocrisy." [88] Arnold concluded that psychological manipulation "has not been a unifying force and I have now come to the belief that moral principles firmly believed in as a matter of faith are essential to freedom in any society." [89] This change of attitude toward moral principles is also evident in Arnold's recently published autobiography in which he commented on the "realistic" attitude of British and American businessmen who felt it necessary to establish ties with Hitler's economic cartels. "Realistic thinking that conflicts with moral principles," he asserted, "always leads to the wrong conclusion. Such realistic thinking is not realistic at all." [90]

In recent years, Arnold also witnessed the growth of moral principles with humanitarian purposes. He saw in President Johnson's Great Society platform a "moral principle which, if followed, will make us rich." This principle "consists in the assertion that it is the duty of the government to follow an economic policy that requires the full use of the productive capacity of the nation." [91] Arnold regarded the Great Society programs, and the expansionary economics on which they were based, as a moral commitment to his long-standing humanitarian goal of maximum production and distribution of goods in society.

Moreover, this moral commitment does not, like the creeds of the 1930s, impose impossible standards on human nature and practical organizations. "Economic sacrifice," contended Arnold, "is something that cannot be expected in an economy based on private enterprise in time of peace. But the policy announced by the President [Johnson] requires no economic sacrifice. It will add to the profits of private enterprise instead of taking them away." [92] Arnold seemed to have reached the conclusion that moral principles expressed in terms of human need, and taking account of the imperfections of human nature, can be formulated and *followed*. During the 1930s he doubted that such ideals would be formulated and, therefore, conceived of all ideals as symbols to be manipulated rather than precepts to be followed. He later learned to trust ideals more and the manipulation of symbols less. The evolution of Arnold's attitudes toward moral values marks a substantial change but not a *reversal* of his earlier views. He retained the greatest admiration for a political leader who could get results by manipulating symbols, of which Lyndon Johnson's political skill in securing domestic legislation was a perfect example. However, Arnold no longer accepted manipulation as a positive value in its own right; it is a serious danger unless controlled by humanitarian purposes and social tolerance. The most accurate conclusion is that Arnold's early enthusiasm for opportunistic manipulation has proven to be less important in his scheme of values than commitment to humanitarian principles.

Although committed to certain principles, Arnold saw no point in constructing elaborate philosophical definitions of "the good." Rather, he professed a simple humanitarian creed expressed in terms of maximum production and distribution of goods in an atmosphere of social tolerance. When asked in 1962 what philosophy he would recommend to a young man getting started in today's world, he replied with his usual clarity and simplicity, "A philosophy might consist in not being too selfish in his efforts, not too materialistic, recognizing that there are great humanitarian objectives in society." [93] The philosophically inclined have always found it impossible to obtain pontifical moral pronouncements from Arnold. If asked where one should look to find moral truth, he would probably have replied, "At the bottom of a well, I would say. That's where truth lies." [94]

# NOTES

[1] Thurman Arnold, *Fair Fights and Foul* (New York: Harcourt, Brace & World, Inc., 1965), pp. 5, 6.

[2] Ibid., p. 17  [3] p. 18  [4] ibid.  [5] p. 19  [6] p. 20.

[7] Ibid.  [8] p. 28  [9] p. 33  [10] ibid.  [11] p. 32.

[12] Joseph Alsop and Robert Kintner, "Trustbuster: The Folklore of Thurman Arnold," *Saturday Evening Post,* vol. 212 (August 12, 1939), p. 30.

[13] Ibid.  [14] p. 33.

[15] Arnold, *Fair Fights and Foul*, pp. 33–35.

[16] Alsop and Kintner, "Trustbuster," p. 30.

[17] Arnold, *Fair Fights and Foul*, p. 35. Arnold's writings at West Virginia dealt mainly with technical or specialized topics, e.g., "The Collection of Judicial Statistics in West Virginia," *West Virginia Law Quarterly,* vol. 36 (February 1930), pp. 184–90; "Contempt-Evasion of Criminal Process as Contempt of Court," *West Virginia Law Quarterly,* vol. 34 (February 1928), pp. 188–92. His broad philosophy of law emerged in his writings at Yale.  [18] Ibid.  [19] pp. 37–68.

[20] Alsop and Kintner, "Trustbuster," p. 30.

[21] Arnold, *Fair Fights and Foul*, pp. 131–32.

[22] Ibid., p. 132  [23] pp. 134–35  [24] p. 135  [25] pp. 135–36  [26] p. 136.

27 Corwin D. Edwards, "Thurman Arnold and the Antitrust Laws," *Political Science Quarterly,* vol. 58 (September 1943), p. 339.  28 Ibid., p. 353.

29 Arnold, *Fair Fights and Foul,* p. 156.  30 Ibid., p. 159.

31 Louis Cassels, "Arnold, Fortas, Porter and Prosperity," *Harper's,* vol. 203 (November 1951), p. 65.

32 Arnold, *Fair Fights and Foul,* p. 190.

33 Cassels, "Arnold, Fortas, Porter and Prosperity," pp. 65–66.

34 Ibid., p. 66  35 p. 67.

36 Arnold, *Fair Fights and Foul,* pp. 215–16.  37 Ibid., p. 217.

38 Cassels, "Arnold, Fortas, Porter and Prosperity," p. 62.

39 Thurman Arnold, *The Symbols of Government* (New Haven: Yale University Press, 1935), p. 267.  40 Ibid., p. 30.

41 Ibid., *The Folklore of Capitalism* (New Haven: Yale University Press, 1937), pp. 16–17.  42 Ibid., p. 156  43 p. 157.

44 Ibid., *Symbols of Government,* pp. 47–48.

45 Ibid., "Theories about Economic Theory," *Annals of the American Academy of Political and Social Science,* vol. 172 (March 1934), p. 36.

46 Ibid., *Folklore of Capitalism,* pp. 56–57.  47 Ibid., p. 57  48 ibid.  49 p. 55.

50 Thurman Arnold et al., *The Future of Democratic Capitalism* (Philadelphia: University of Pennsylvania Press, 1950), pp. 1–2.

51 Arnold, *Folklore of Capitalism,* p. 180.

52 Max Lerner, "The Shadow World of Thurman Arnold," *Yale Law Journal,* vol. 47 (March 1938), p. 689.

53 Thurman Arnold, "The Folklore of Mr. Hook—A Reply," *University of Chicago Law Review,* vol. 5 (April 1938), p. 353.

54 Ibid., *Folklore of Capitalism,* p. 179.  55 Ibid., p. 349.

56 Ibid., "Review of *Conflicting Penal Theories in Statutory Criminal Law* by Mabel A. Elliot," *Illinois Law Review,* vol. 26 (February 1932), p. 722.

57 Ibid., "Theories about Economic Theory," p. 28.

58 Ibid., *Symbols of Government,* pp. 77–78.

59 Ibid., p. 77  60 p. 81  61 p. 89  62 p. 88.

63 Ibid., "The Jurisprudence of Edward S. Robinson," *Yale Law Journal,* vol. 46 (June 1937), p. 1282.

64 Ibid., *Symbols of Government,* p. 103.

65 Ibid., "The Folklore of Mr. Hook—A Reply," p. 351.  66 Ibid.

67 Ibid., "Law Enforcement—An Attempt at Social Dissection," *Yale Law Journal,* vol. 42 (November 1932), pp. 23–24.

68 Lerner, "The Shadow World of Thurman Arnold," p. 688.

69 Arnold, *Folklore of Capitalism,* p. 30.

70 Lerner, "The Shadow World of Thurman Arnold," p. 695.

71 Joseph Featherstone, "The Machiavelli of the New Deal," *New Republic,* vol. 153 (August 7, 1965), p. 23.

72 Arnold, *Folklore of Capitalism,* p. 138.  73 Ibid.

74 Ibid., *Symbols of Government,* pp. 232–33.

75 Ibid., "Theories about Economic Theory," p. 36.  76 Ibid., p. 29  77 ibid.

78 Ibid., *Folklore of Capitalism,* pp. 341–42.

79 Ibid., *Symbols of Government,* p. 259.

80 Ibid., p. 263  81 p. 266  82 p. 263.

83 Ibid., *Folklore of Capitalism,* pp. 137–38.

84 Ibid., *Symbols of Government,* p. 264.

85 Richard Hofstadter, *The American Political Tradition* (New York: Vintage Books, 1961), p. 307.

86 Featherstone, "The Machiavelli of the New Deal," p. 24.

87 Lerner, "The Shadow World of Thurman Arnold," p. 702.

88 Thurman Arnold, *Selections from the Letters and Legal Papers of Thurman Arnold,* collected by Victor H. Kramer (Washington, D.C.: Merkle Press Inc., 1961), p. 55.   89 Ibid.

90 Ibid., *Fair Fights and Foul,* p. 84   91 Ibid., p. 285   92 pp. 284–85.

93 Ibid., "Advice to a Young Man," *Changing Times* (June 1962), p. 20.

94 Ibid.

CHAPTER III

# SYMBOLS AND INSTITUTIONS

Thurman Arnold's most important contribution to American social and political thought was his theory of the interrelationships between social symbols and institutions. By institutions, Arnold meant human organizations that give prestige, morale, and purpose to their members. Social symbols refer both to social ideals and to the many ceremonies by which society dramatizes these ideals.

Arnold did not view ideals in terms of transcendence, but in terms of human organizations. He asserted that "philosophies have no meaning apart from organizations." It is fruitless, he believed, to argue about whether the philosophy or the organization comes first. It is sufficient to say that "they grow up together and each molds the other." [1] Arnold described institutions and their ideals as "living organisms" similar in many ways to human personalities. They are ". . . moulded by habit, shaken by emotional conflicts . . . constantly making good resolutions . . . and never quite understanding themselves or the part they are actually playing because of the necessary illusions with which they must surround themselves to preserve their prestige and self-respect." [2]

Men engaged in continuous cooperative activity, Arnold contended, develop organizations. These are held together by discipline, habits, and morale which taken together may be described as the organization's "personality" or "character." Once it is formed, the personality of an organization "is as difficult to change as the habits of an individual." [3] Moreover, institutional personalities, like human personalities, are made up of "a whole bundle of contradictory roles." Thus a business corporation is supposed to make money for its stockholders by hard bargaining and at the same time is supposed to represent the best in morals and ethics. [4]

Just as ideals hold human personality together, so social symbols maintain cohesion within institutions. A commonly accepted creed, a set of institutional habits by which men cooperate automatically and unconsciously, and a mythological tradition are absolutely necessary. Without them, "organization can be maintained only by force, and force cannot be continued long because it is too exhausting." [5]

Arnold compared social symbols to folklore or superstition. When institutions are functioning effectively it is the power of superstition rather than the power of reason which holds them together. [6] The cohesive and morale-building functions of folklore, however, depend on its being accepted literally. In 1937, Arnold noted that no one thought of sound principles of law and economics as folklore. They were considered inescapable truths, as the only method of an ordered society. All vital folklore must be so accepted. The moment it is recognized as folklore, it "descends to the place of poetry or fairy tales which affect us only in our romantic moments." [7]

Although ideals and institutions are related in common development, they remain separate in two important ways: ideals do not *describe* or *guide* the actual workings of institutions. Arnold limited the function of ideals to building morale and confidence in human organizations. An efficiently organized society, he asserted, is one where "ideals protect its institutions from criticism and permit them to function with confidence without either guiding them or interfering with them." [8] This requires the development of *separate* institutions which do not collide with each other. One of these institutions is concerned with "the practical organization of men into productive groups. The other is concerned with the embodiment of spiritual ideals. "Where the spiritual government allows the practical institutions the most freedom, there we find the greatest progress and development." [9]

"The logical content of creeds," Arnold argued, "never realistically describes the institutions to which the creeds are attached." [10] Moreover, creeds do not control the actual workings of institutions. Men in control of political or business organizations do not use the philosophical literature of law and economics in their daily operations. "They, nevertheless, take great comfort in the fact that it is being produced in order to give stability to the . . . ideals on which their prestige is based." [11]

Whereas most thinkers would agree that institutions seldom live up to their ideals, few go as far as Arnold in consigning theory and practice to separate categories. Arnold's position should not be confused with the more commonly held belief that although institutions cannot completely live up to their ideals, they can *approach* those ideals with effort. Arnold's contention was that effective institutions must find ways to keep their theories conveniently separated from their practices: "Social institutions require faiths and dreams to give them morale. They need to escape from these faiths and dreams in order to progress . . . governing institutions must pretend to symmetry, moral beauty, and logic in order to maintain their prestige and power. To actually govern, they must constantly violate those principles in hidden and covert ways." [12]

For this reason, Arnold believed that devotion to consistency is harmful to practical organizations. Those who try to make institutions live up to their ideals have a destructive rather than a constructive effect. "The history of human organization," he observed, "is strewn with the wreckage caused by people who tried honestly and sincerely to follow the logical implications of accepted doctrine." [13]

Because Americans have more difficulty than, for example, the British in living with the inconsistencies between ideals and institutions, it has been necessary to create the appearance of consistency. Sometimes a "simple ceremony" is all that is required to reconcile ideals with institutional practice. For example, equality and democracy in hierarchical industrial organizations are represented by employer-employee banquets and by literature in the Horatio Alger tradition. [14]

Simple ceremonies will not suffice when disparities between theories and practice become too obvious to be concealed easily. In such times of spiritual confusion there is a proliferation of philosophical literature that seeks to reconcile inconsistencies: "When symbols or beliefs have no relation to what men see before them . . . men must drown their observations in doctrine and philosophy . . . mystical literature increases by leaps and bounds, becoming more and more abstract as it grows." [15] Thus, Justice Sutherland's philosophical doctrine that minimum wage legislation for women destroyed their freedom of contract was a natural outgrowth of a period of spiritual conflict.[16]

The ceremonies and doctrines of the conservatives, however, are seldom convincing to the radicals who develop their own set of ideals to justify change. Philosophical learning, and the public debate that accompanies it, serves each side by creating enthusiasm and quieting doubt. Such debate is ceremonial in nature and "can have nothing to do with the actual practical analysis of facts." [17] Political debate, Arnold concluded, "is in reality a series of cheers in which each side strives to build up its own morale." [18]

It is clear that Arnold was sharply at odds with the libertarian-Jeffersonian assumptions concerning the function of public debate in a free society. According to these assumptions, public debate informs citizens, develops their capacity for critical thought, and influences their final decisions. Arnold's view attacked these assumptions. Political opinions, he believed, grow out of loyalty to organizations, which, in turn, is a product of habit and custom, not of reason and deliberation. Public debate, therefore, neither informs citizens nor determines their political preferences. These are predetermined by habitual loyalties to organizations which give their members prestige and morale. Public debate does not operate to inform the public, but rather to "reconcile the spiritual conflict within an organization and to attract followers to that organization by appealing to their prejudices." [19] Paradoxically, although Arnold decried the assumptions of the libertarian-Jeffersonian tradition, he was a strong supporter of the freedoms of speech and press. This derived partly from his commitment to a tolerant humanitarian society (see Chapter II) and partly from his conviction that ceremonial philosophy and debate are as inevitable in the drama of human existence as are fancy clothes and tablecloths.

Arnold's conception of the relation between ideals and institutions was derived largely from his observations of American society in the period preceding the Depression. He noted that the prevailing economic creeds gave business organizations freedom of action and at the same time protected them from their enemies. Although businessmen could use the doctrine of *laissez faire* to ward off governmental regulation, they were not required to follow the doctrine to its logical conclusions. Thus, while *laissez faire* economists preached international free trade, *laissez faire* businessmen insisted on letting protective tariffs alone.[20]

The prevailing doctrines of free trade provided a safe context within which public debate could take place. Reformers usually limited themselves to demands that business organizations live up to their own ideals which, observed Arnold, was "an essentially impossible task." The battle over principles, therefore, remained at a level which did not "permit the spiritual government seriously to interfere with the operation of the great temporal institutions." When reformers succeeded in passing antitrust laws and other measures, business institutions easily adapted themselves "leaving older reformers disillusioned . . . and a newer set carrying on the banner." [21]

Probably the most important creed supporting business supremacy in the pre-Depression period was the notion that private corporations were individuals. These organizations were known to dominate the distribution of necessities such as light, heat, housing, and transportation; yet economic and legal theory viewed them as "rugged individuals" rather than private governments.[22] In actual practice, contended Arnold, business organizations were much more like disciplined armies than individuals. Business discipline was expressed in terms of hard work, instant obedience, and loyal cooperation with superior officers. "The penalty for lack of obedience and loyalty was discharge from the business army." [23] Although the ideal of the corporation as a "rugged individual" did not describe the actual workings of private organizations, it vested them with power and prestige: "The ideal that a great corporation is endowed with the rights and prerogatives of a free individual is as essential to the acceptance of corporate rule in temporal affairs as was the ideal of the divine right of kings in an earlier day." [24] Men come to believe that their personal freedom is tied up with the freedom of private corporations from regulation. Similarly, men in the Middle Ages believed that their salvation depended on reverence and support of great ecclesiastical organizations.[25]

The ideal of individualism, Arnold said, grew out of our pioneer civilization which both practiced and preached the independence of the free man from central authority. The subsequent growth of corporate organizations in which most men were employees and a few at the top were dictators contradicted the individualistic pioneer philosophy. Yet new mechanical techniques demanded new organizations in which work became specialized so that no man could operate by himself. To reconcile this contradiction, the philosophical doctrine was developed that corporations were individuals. Thus, the pioneer ideal became the "mystical philosophy that put the corporate organization ahead of the governmental organization in prestige and power, by identifying it with the individual." [26]

Arnold cited the theory behind the antitrust laws as a leading example of the personification of corporations. The theory was that corporations were not organizations to be controlled but individuals who must be punished if they did not compete fairly. Like individuals, some monopolies were reasonable while others were unreasonable. This misconception led to great confusion in enforcement of the antitrust laws. The result, Arnold said, "was the same as if the courts in time of war should lay down and clarify the principles of what were reasonable and unreasonable combinations of troops." [27] Effective regulation of large combinations of corporations was impossible as long as the folklore of the times conceived of them as individuals rather than as disciplined organizations. The antitrust laws actually became "the great bulwark of defense of these organizations against any regulation whatever." They offered an "escape valve" through which the energies of reformers might be spent and, at the same time, allowed the great corporations to go on undisturbed.[28]

Viewed from another perspective, the antitrust laws were an example of a ceremony which reconciles the conflict between an ideal and a practical need. The ideal of rugged individualism conflicted with the growing need of Americans for mass-produced goods. It became necessary to develop a procedure to attack bigness on moral grounds and, at the same time, not seriously to interfere with the large corporations needed for mass production. The antitrust laws provided the answer for Americans who "felt the need of great organizations, and at the same time had to deny them a place in the moral and logical ideology of the social structure." [29]

In times of prosperity the antitrust laws reinforced the image of corporations as competing individuals. In times of economic adversity the same function was performed by what Arnold referred to as the "ritual of corporate reorganization." Arnold became familiar with the reorganizations which accompanied corporate insolvency as a trial examiner for the Securities and Exchange Commission during the mid-1930s. The central idea of the ritual, according to Arnold, was the personification of corporations as individuals who must pay their debts or atone for not paying by giving up all their property. Of course, the great corporations were not "property" that could be bought or sold. Their value consisted of their organization, discipline, and morale. These institutional habits, commented Arnold, could no more be "bought" as tangible property than the Republican party in New York could "buy" the successful Vare machine in Philadelphia so that they could beat Tammany Hall.[30]

Corporate reorganizations actually had little to do with individuals paying their debts or atoning for not paying them. They were in reality political struggles between contending groups for the control of great organizations. The contenders planned their campaigns in accordance with the accepted symbols of debts, credits, and sales. The drama of reorganization was played before a court. On the judicial stage, "no one was permitted to talk naturally about the facts of financial life and politics."[31]

But if one looked behind the judicial drama of an execution sale, he discovered a struggle between *sub rosa* political machines "using patronage, demagogic appeals, and all the favorite devices of such machines to influence and control the vast unorganized mass of individual creditors."[32] As in most political campaigns, said Arnold, the "ins" had the advantage over the "outs." The "outs" used the same symbols in their campaigns as are found in a national election; they charged the "ins" with corruption, failure to balance the budget, and dominance by selfish financial interests. The "ins" replied by charging the "outs" with being radicals and advancing "unsound" economic schemes. And both parties always expressed intense concern for the "little fellow." As soon as the creditors had elected their leadership (usually the "ins"), the contenders stopped attacking each other and accepted the chosen administration. "The voter had about the same knowledge of what was going on as in the ordinary municipal election."[33]

The "ritual of corporate reorganization" was significant in that it gave the *sub rosa* machines within private organizations great freedom to maneuver. The folklore that personified corporations also gave them great freedom of action in taxing and spending.

The folklore of the day, Arnold said, protected private expenditures, no matter how fantastic, from criticism or investigation. Such spending was considered that of a free individual spending his own money. The same folklore hampered government spending by associating it with the unpleasant symbol of the tax gatherer.[34]

One method by which private organizations collected revenue was by offering opportunities for investment. When an investor lost his money it was not considered a tax but a lesson to him to listen to the advice of sound bankers. When the public generally lost money, it was still not considered a tax but rather "a regrettable lack of judgment on the part of the public." [35]

By means of this folklore, business activity came to be associated with the pleasant symbol of the individual buying freely in the market place. Government activity became associated with the unpleasant symbol of compulsory taxation. So odious were the symbols surrounding government spending that the collection of income taxes "became a combat . . . in which 45,000 registered lawyers and tax accountants were pitted against some 2,800 persons employed by the government." A respected business leader like J. P. Morgan could remark, "If the government cannot collect its taxes a man is a fool to pay them." No respectable person, however, could make the statement that if a bank is unable to collect its notes, a debtor is a fool to pay them.[36]

The prevailing folklore caused people to prefer the services of the great industrial organizations and to distrust those provided by the government. Rents, light, heat, and transportation were regarded as services purchased voluntarily while police protection, libraries, and parks were paid for involuntarily by taxes. The real danger to the income of the small man was, therefore, taxes—not prices.[37]

The folklore of the pre-Depression period, Arnold concluded, operated to produce two kinds of institutions: one called "business" concerned itself with the practical matters of building cities, distributing goods, and holding control over the lives of millions; the other called "government" was concerned with the embodiment of spiritual ideals. Government was limited to its spiritual role by the judicial system, which reflected the view of most Americans that the government should confine itself to preaching.[38]

The neat separation of practical and spiritual institutions worked extremely well before the Depression. "This philosophy," observed Arnold, "gave enough freedom for opportunistic action to our temporal industrial government to make it one of the marvels of the world in productive efficiency." [39] Arnold was deeply impressed with what practical organizations could achieve with the aid of a favorable set of ideals. The folklore of capitalism, he said, made businessmen the least hampered group, and therefore the group with the highest morale in American society. "It is out of that group that our discoveries and achievements in human organization have come." [40]

For this reason, private government "was impregnable from the attacks of reformers so long as it continued to keep order in the industrial world." [41] Privately maintained order and prosperity broke down with the advent of the Depression. A large gap appeared between the needs of the American people and the ability of private government to fill them. Men were no longer assured of jobs, housing, food, and clothing —much less a high standard of living. When government moved to fill this gap, it was met by the mighty impact of prevailing ideals which cramped all its attempts to develop new organizations and techniques. Creeds that had made possible the creation of mighty business organizations now obstructed the development of new governmental organizations struggling to fill social and economic gaps. Arnold stated that his purpose was not to attack the "folklore of capitalism," but to explain the ideological difficulties it creates for new organizations attempting to provide the security no longer provided by "the industrial feudalism." [42]

The great difficulty, according to Arnold, is that the mythical ideals which allowed business to be practical and efficient behind the scenes make it exceedingly difficult for government to be efficient at all. During times of spiritual confusion like the Depression, unrealistic ideals become standards by which new organizations are judged. In such an atmosphere, it is impossible to make evaluations in terms of practical performance.

The great battle in the 1930s did not concern the practical effects of governmental programs, but whether or not capitalism was worth preserving. Practical plans had to be tested by economic theorists "who looked at each practical measure through the spectacles of economic abstractions in order not to be confused by immediate objectives." Child labor laws had to be debated, not on the basis of the desirability of children working but in terms of "its effect on the American home in ten years, if it were followed to its logical conclusion." [43] A choice among practical alternatives was made impossible by "the holy war between Capitalism, Communism, and Facism." Soil conservation and crop insurance programs could never be judged practically so long as they were viewed in terms of the alien creeds of Communism and Fascism.

During the spiritual confusion of the Depression period, it was assumed that principles were more to be trusted than organizations. Organizations might stray, but principles endured forever. Such a philosophical climate made it exceedingly difficult for new organizations to get started. "The greater the philosophical learning of the time," said Arnold, "the more difficult it is for new organizations to find a place in the logical structure of government." [44]

The emphasis on principles rather than the practical performance of organizations causes an ideological rigidity which makes gradual and orderly change more difficult. The rise of revolutionary theorists, said Arnold, "is generally a direct result of a devoted belief of conservatives that there should be no compromise with principle." [45] Compromise becomes more difficult when debate is shifted from the uncertainties of practical affairs to the certainties of opposing schools of learning. Learned philosophical discourses rarely change opinions. Rather, they give greater certainty and rigidity to existing ideological divisions.

A central part of the "holy war" between principles in times of stress is what Arnold referred to as the myth of "the thinking man." "The thinking man," he observed, is "the gentleman who accepts sound and rejects unsound principles." Education, a free press, and unlimited public discussion are aids to his unemotional and unbiased decisions.[46] The modern symbol of "the thinking man" responding to reason has replaced the medieval symbol of "the believing man" responding to faith. These different symbols, however, represent the same social phenomenon: the application of universal principles as weapons against new forms of social organization. In both cases a Devil is discovered who is leading the righteous away from sound principles. In the Middle Ages, the "heretic" was the incarnation of the Devil; in modern times, the role is played by the "demagogue." A Hell is also invented as punishment for accepting unsound principles. The eternal fire and brimstone of the Middle Ages served the same purpose as the specter of inflation, destruction of individual initiative, and bureaucratic controls serve in America. Finally, a priesthood is needed to prescribe sound principles to which righteous men will respond. The clergy of the Middle Ages served this purpose as do the respectable lawyers and economists of modern capitalism.[47]

The spiritual conflict between the practical needs of a people and their prevailing ideals shapes the new organizations which arise to fill in the gaps left by old organizations. Where a practical need is not accepted as moral or legitmate, undercover or *sub rosa* organizations will arise to meet the need. These organizations "will be . . . tolerated as a necessary evil, in the same way that the Church accepted the existence of the Devil." [48] During the prohibition experiment, for example, a vast organization of bootleggers became necessary to meet the demand for liquor. These organizations were publicly denounced and a few of their leaders put in jail; however, the moral censure never went so far as to stop the supply of alcohol.[49]

Arnold explained the existence of political machines in a similar fashion. As long as the provision of a certain amount of material security was not considered a legitimate function of government, the task was performed by *sub rosa* political machines run by relatively unscrupulous persons. Arnold cited the following comment by a member of a corrupt, large city, political machine who dispensed favors to some thirty families: "These people do not want to vote for gangsters. But they know that if I am out of power they will be turned over to a cruel system of charity. Can you blame them if they . . . (do not) vote for an administration which . . . (tells) them that they should willingly suffer indignity for the sake of decreasing the burden on large taxpayers. . . ." [50] "It is therefore natural," concluded Arnold, "that the country whose theories of government are the most unrealistic in the world should develop the greatest and most powerful *sub rosa* political machinery." [51] When a governmental function finally comes to be accepted as legitimate, undercover organizations disappear and a more scrupulous class of people comes to power.

New organizations must necessarily be nonrespectable at first, yet they are the most important force generating social change. "Probably the only way in which mythologies actually change," observed Arnold, "is through the rise to power of a new class whose traditional heroes are of a different mold." [52] When a ruling class associated with older institutions ceases to distribute goods according to the demands of a people, a new class appears to meet the demand. The new class is looked down upon at first, but gradually creates a mythology of its own. Finally, this new creed comes to be accepted as the standard of respectability.[53]

During the Middle Ages, for example, merchants and bankers had no prestige in a society based on feudalism and chivalry. When the practical need for banking and credit began to be felt, only the despised Jewish moneylenders could fill it. Later the ideals and practices of this nonrespectable class became the standard of respectability embodied in the successful businessman. The governmental organizations of the 1930s, said Arnold, found themselves in the position of the medieval moneylenders. They were under pressure to fill practical needs neglected by the older social order, but met with the same "theological opposition" which confronted the growth of private banking in the Middle Ages.[54]

Not only must new organizations pass through a period of nonrespectability, they must also pass through a period of confusion and fumbling; and private business organizations are no exception. United States Steel, said Arnold, "is a gradual development from complete anarchy. . . ."[55] These organizations, however, were protected in their growing stages by a set of symbols which allowed them to make mistakes. Corporations were individuals who could do as they chose with their property, whereas the new governmental organizations of the 1930s had no set of symbols to protect them from criticism. When they erred, it was considered a tax on posterity. The standards of the day, said Arnold, required "that a *governmental* organization should be mature when it is born."[56]

New organizations must go through a difficult period of self-justification before they can make practical management their chief concern. Legislation which creates these new organizations must be a kind of political platform which authorizes a new program. Its purpose is not to provide a detailed blueprint for the future, but to get a new idea accepted and a new organization started: "The first function of such legislation can be only to give an organization a respectable place in which to begin the necessary fumbling which all growing institutions have to go through with."[57] When the new activity is finally accepted as a commonplace thing for government to do, "management becomes more important than logic, and the inherent organizing ability of a people gradually gets under way while intellectual conservatives and radicals battle over something else." [58]

Arnold's emphasis on the confusion and fumbling of new organizations is closely related to his theory of social change. He is strongly committed to gradual orderly change as opposed to violent revolutionary change. "The only path of *orderly* social change," Arnold commented, "leads through a confusion of principles." [59] The sudden imposition of clearcut and logical principles is usually accompanied by violence. When a nation becomes so devoted to a single ideal that it rejects all competing values, it becomes cruel and intolerant. "Thus, it appears that the more illogical the process of social change is, the less disorder and repression accompany it. By proceeding in different directions at the same time, the ancient habits of thought are preserved while molding them to new needs." [60]

The operation of conflicting ideological forces in times of social change, observed Arnold, is reflected in the confused picture of the New Deal legislation. The National Recovery Act, for example, "unified under its slogans more of the contradictory ideals which were generally accepted than any other piece of legislation." [61] The Social Security Act also represented all of the conflicting ideals of the time. The Act was like a pension; it was like insurance; it recognized the doctrine of states rights, and the notion that government should not interfere with business.[62] The Act was based on the assumption that "we could afford to go through the period of confused bookkeping necessary while the new institution . . . struggled to get itself into working order." The importance of the Social Security Act was "its acknowledgment of a social obligation dressed in the ideas of a time before such a social obligation was recognized." [63]

Arnold contended that when new governmental programs are initiated they must be dressed in the prevailing symbols of the time, even though these symbols do not accurately describe the operations of the programs. Thus, when the national government undertook new programs for the distribution of food, power, or the financial support of businesses in economic distress, it had to pretend that it was an individual buying and selling in a competitive market. This symbolism was necessary for it to obtain freedom of action.[64]

Arnold believed that the development of institutions involved both technical and psychological problems. His chief concern was with the latter. Institutional reform, he maintained, "must be attempted with something like the same point of view with which a trained psychiatrist reforms an individual." [65] This point of view recognizes that institutions have what Arnold liked to call a "subconscious mind." By this he meant that the moralistic rationalizations of institutions rarely describe or explain their actual workings. Arnold was of the opinion that the psychiatric approach to institutional reform avoids the misconception that caused reformers to fail in the past, i.e., that government must be logical and consistent. Reformers must come to accept the irrational motive forces of politics just as psychiatrists have come to accept the irrational motive forces of the human personality.

The acceptance of irrational creeds and symbols opens the door for the objective study of these powerful forces and their eventual use as a means of social control: "Men are coming to realize that political government is necessarily a dramatic spectacle, that games are really important in the growth and development of institutions, and that these games can be controlled." [66]

Arnold wished to exert social control for the purpose of widespread distribution of the nation's wealth. If, by the manipulation of symbols, Americans could become as enthusiastic about achieving this goal as they have been about achieving victory in war, their accomplishments would be unprecedented.

Many of the psychological problems afflicting new institutions, Arnold thought, are directly traceable to the attitudes of the more educated segment of the American population, although there is no doubt about the intelligence and good intentions of this group. Moreover, it constitutes "the only class from which orderly change without violent social dislocation can be hoped," yet it is this class which is most enslaved by prevailing symbols: ". . . they are the very ones who are most readily prevented from reacting in a common-sense or humanitarian way, because they are the group which has been doing the reading and thinking, i.e., worshiping in connection with existing organizations." [67]

These educated, respectable people, believing in consistency of principle and practice, are repelled by the opportunistic use of symbols. Control of these techniques, therefore, falls into the hands of less scrupulous people called "politicians." When respectable people learn to accept and use irrational symbols, the quality of political leadership improves. Grosser and more unpleasant forms of political chicanery disappear.[68] Arnold concluded that if more members of the educated, respectable class in America would learn to appreciate the psychiatric approach to symbols and the political techniques that go with it, the process of social change would become more orderly and humane.

Arnold denied that his psychiatric approach is a universal truth in which all men should believe. He saw it as a desirable attitude only for those who study and manage governmental institutions. Most citizens will continue to think in terms of a religion of government rather than a science of government. Neither of these viewpoints, insisted Arnold, is more "true" than the other; both are needed at different times. "When . . . a person needs cheer or decoration it is well to call in an artist. When he requires a diagnosis, he needs a physician." [69] Thus, Arnold believed that the inspirational ceremonial orientation is just as "real" a part of life as the objective practical orientation. He does not wish to unite these two spheres but rather to bring them into a kind of peaceful coexistence. In Great Britain, Arnold pointed out, relatively peaceful coexistence between these two spheres allows royal ceremonies to be carried on enthusiastically while practical men are free to direct state affairs behind the scenes.

Because creeds and ceremonies play such an important part in human affairs, new institutions must develop a mythology of their own if they are to gain a respectable place in society. This mythology cannot be a new and unfamiliar formulation. It must be "selected out of the mass of conflicting ideals which exist in the culture by a process not unlike the development of language." [70]

Arnold's writings over the years are not explicit or consistent concerning the content of the new creed that organizations of the future will employ. This is partly because he believes that no one can accurately predict the creeds of the future, and partly because creeds must be opportunistically adapted to the practical needs of the times. In *The Symbols of Government,* however, Arnold did allow himself to speculate concerning the creed of the future. A new humanitarian creed, he observed, whose axiom is that man works for his fellowman is appearing all over the world. This creed is no more descriptive than the capitalistic creed that man works for his own selfish interests. The important point is that it promises to bring order and morale to new organizations. In America, new nonprofit organizations are "arising out of confusion rather than revolution" and are rapidly growing in prestige as new governmental obligations are recognized in areas that were formerly reserved to private charity. Writing in 1935, Arnold noted that "the greatest employer of labor in the country is not an industrial baron, but Harry Hopkins, a social worker." [71]

Writing two years later in *The Folklore of Capitalism,* Arnold was must less explicit in describing the creed of the future. A new creed was being born, he said, which had no formulas but was represented vaguely by the personality of Franklin Roosevelt. It expressed ". . . the current distrust of old myths and the belief that the government has a new role to play in providing for security of individuals in their jobs and in the distribution of goods." [72]

Three decades have passed since Arnold made his trenchant observations concerning symbols and institutions in his two major works, *The Symbols of Government* and *The Folklore of Capitalism.* The vast economic changes which occurred over this period caused him to modify some of these observations substantially.

The ideals and symbols which stood in the way of government regulation of business, Arnold noted not long before his death, have all but disappeared. He felt that his observations on "the personification of corporations" and "the ritual of corporate reorganization" were "largely obsolete today." The vast regulatory bureaus of government had "lost their radical tinge" and had "obtained an almost invulnerable place in the hierarchy of our institutions." [73]

Nevertheless, Arnold pointed out that many of the psychological problems faced by government bureaus in the 1930s remained to plague them in the 1960s. In *The Folklore of Capitalism,* he observed that institutions, like human personalities, "become very much like the little pictures which men have of them." Thus, if a government organization is viewed as a "useless bureaucracy," those who work for it will come to resemble that image.[74] In 1965, he noted that these negative public attitudes about bureaucracy and bureaucrats remain as a "psychological millstone" around the neck of government operations. Only at the top echelons of government service does an "atmosphere of dignity and prestige" exist. Below this level, government career men are regarded as "mere bureaucrats." Arnold observed that the housing provided for government workers remains a symbol of the public's disrespect for bureaucracy. "Artistic decoration of these stark, boxlike structures is absolutely prohibited." He concluded that "An atmosphere of respect and dignity, in which the government servant can hold up his head, must be . . . created." [75]

Although the symbols which prevented the acceptance of government regulation of business have largely disappeared, Arnold acknowledged that nineteenth-century economic symbols still cause confusion in the area of monetary and fiscal policy. These symbols center around the idea that the wealth of a nation consists of its money supply rather than its productive capacity. This idea has made educated voters the "prisoners of an obsolete bookkeeping system" based on the notion that "the production of goods should be cut down to fit the supply of money and credit instead of increasing the amount of money and credit to fit the expanding industrial capacity of our productive plants." [76] Under such a system of bookkeeping, the government is prevented from effectively using the nation's resources for a wide variety of badly needed public services. The old system of bookkeeping was well suited to the nineteenth century when our productive capacity was not great enough to support public projects without the danger of inflation. It is, however, badly outmoded in the 1960s "when our productive capacity is so great that only 75 per cent of it can be absorbed by the purchasing power created by private credit. . . ." [77] The huge expenditures of the Vietnamese war did not alter Arnold's conviction that our inadequate supply of public services is not due to a physical lack of capacity but to a psychological lack of determination.[78]

The tendency of contemporary symbols to regard national wealth in terms of money supply not only blinds Americans to their unused productive capacity but also prevents them from recognizing that things without a dollar value on the marketplace are nevertheless assets of incalculable value. Thus, the government can help finance vast private housing projects because future rents or purchase installments will pay for them. But the government "cannot build schools and hospitals, preserve our water supply, improve recreational areas, or train doctors, because such programs are not self-liquidating in money terms." Spending for items whose return cannot be expressed in dollars is considered "an economic sin and a burden on the taxpayer and leads hell-bent to inflation." [79]

To free our monetary and fiscal policy from nineteenth-century symbols, Arnold wrote, "We need a set of words that will convey the idea

79

that the wealth of a nation consists of its capacity to produce goods, that programs for the public welfare that cannot be translated into monetary terms are nevertheless assets of incalculable value." [80] He believed that the slogan of balancing the economic budget rather than the fiscal budget conveys these ideas. The slogan means that our national productive capacity should be balanced against our demands for necessities such as schools, public works, water conservation, and health. Legislative programs should be based on this formula which makes money supply a means rather than an end.[81] The Full Employment Act of 1946 embodies the policy of balancing the economic budget while the Federal Reserve Board champions the traditional and restrictive policy of balancing the fiscal budget.[82]

According to Arnold, the presidential elections of 1960 and 1964 were historic landmarks in the evolving relationships between symbols and institutions. He saw the 1960 election as a vindication of his prediction in 1935 that symbols would come to be viewed less as logical truths and more as objects for manipulation. The two presidential candidates in 1960 devoted all their efforts to projecting images, and the voters did not object. Arnold believed that "The cynical psychiatric attitude of the voters toward the issues represented a growing distrust of the fundamental economic faiths that had been so powerful a source of frustration during the Great Depression." [83]

In 1964, however, the Republican party decided to have done with campaigns based on images and advocated a return to the fundamental principles of the past. Johnson, in the style of a "devout country preacher," advocated the principle of a moral obligation to the future.[84] The election of 1964, unlike that of 1960, was a contest over principles, and Johnson's victory represented the "rededication of America to a new principle. . . ." [85]

Arnold concluded that the election of 1960 was a "necessary phase" standing between disillusionment with old principles and acceptance of new ones. It proved to be a temporary thing "because government by public relations cannot be a dignified and inspiring form of government." [86] Arnold regarded the public's acceptance of President Johnson's Great Society and War on Poverty slogans as a historic turning point: "The old gods are dead and new gods have taken their place. The ideological warfare between the business community and the administration is ended. In the future, what conflicts may arise will be conflicts about practical matters and not about philosophical differences." [87]

The possibility of public acceptance of a new set of humanitarian symbols clearly brought about a significant change in Arnold's earlier views concerning the relationship between ideals and institutions. Arnold stated, "President Johnson . . . has given us a moral principle which, *if followed*, will make us rich." [88] During the 1930s Arnold's advice was to manipulate principles, not to follow them. The cynicism on which this advice was based seemed to have moderated in recent years. Arnold thought he had found a set of practical *and* publicly acceptable principles which would not be disastrous if followed. He did not insist that these principles must inevitably mislead the voter concerning the actual workings of the economy. Rather the idea expressed in President Johnson's program "enables the educated voter to look at the economy of the scientific revolution without the preconceptions of the past that have prevented him from seeing what is there." [89]

Arnold's unacknowledged but evident abandonment of some of his earlier observations raises the question of whether his major writings during the 1930s are simply tracts for the times, or whether they contain lasting contributions to American social thought. The reader is tempted to adopt the former conclusion upon discovering that Arnold's confident and unqualified generalizations about "principles" turn out to apply only to those principles which are not statements of his own humanitarian values.

Despite their exaggerations, Arnold's early writings made an important contribution to American thought by applying European perspectives to a troubled American society during the 1930s. The perspectives were those of Marx, Mannheim, Pareto, Mosca, and Michels—all of whom viewed social and political philosophy as ideology supporting a ruling group or class (or a challenging group or class), and all of whom related ideological change to the struggle among social groups or classes for dominance. As Sidney Hook has noted, Arnold's description of political behavior is particularly important for America "whose intellectual life has been comparatively unaffected by the writings of Pareto, Michels, and the Marxian critique of ideology." Hook concludes: "Even if he [Arnold] has rediscovered truths that were already known, to have rediscovered them in the context he did—American folkways in economics, law and politics—is a genuine contribution to realistic stocktaking." [90]

Arnold followed the lead of these seminal European thinkers by finding the meaning of political philosophy and debate in the conflicting aspirations of social groups, and by discussing social change, not in terms of specific reforms but in terms of the rise in American society of a new class with new organizations and a new ideology. Using this approach, Arnold was able to give penetrating insights into the significance of a decade in American life characterized by unprecedented challenge to the dominance of business groups and unprecedented opportunity for new social departures.

Arnold is not the only American thinker who has described political philosophy and debate in terms of a group struggle. Arthur F. Bentley made this approach central to his science of politics. Bentley's critique of Marx applies equally to Arnold, i.e., that upon close observation his broadly conceived social "classes" dissolve into a number of smaller groups whose purposes and ideologies are frequently in conflict.[91] Close observation of what Arnold refers to as the "business class," for example, reveals a melange of individual firms, a wide variety of trade associations, and a number of national business groups including the National Association of Manufacturers, the U.S. Chamber of Commerce, the National Federation of Independent Business, and the Committee for Economic Development.[92]

Bentley, however, levels his criticism from a perspective glued to the immediate present. If a broad historical perspective is applied, including in its sweep a comparison of feudal and capitalistic institutions, or a more limited comparison of pre-industrial and post-industrial American institutions, the concept of a business class and ideology assumes greater coherence and social significance. Using such a perspective, Arnold is able to explore the content and impact of a historically derived and generally accepted social ideology that forms part of the limiting context within which group conflict occurs. He describes the way in which this context kept American reformers within the safe confines of business ideals, and reduced their crusades to picturesque but futile episodes.

Bentley ignores the broad historical context of political and social life, except for a brief mention of the "habit background" which conditions the rules of the political game.[93] This self-imposed limitation renders him less helpful than Arnold in explaining certain characteristics of contemporary American society which grow out of generally accepted values and, therefore, remain largely unmoved by group conflict.

One such characteristic of contemporary America has been described in John Kenneth Galbraith's widely discussed book, *The Afflu-*

*ent Society.*[94] The author maintains that "The line which divides our area of wealth from our area of poverty is roughly that which divides privately produced and marketed goods and services from publicly rendered services." [95] Galbraith notes the mounting evidence to support his thesis. While consumption of private consumer goods rises, the needs of large cities for adequate public schools, police protection, internal transportation, clean air, and water become increasingly desperate. Los Angeles provides a "near classic" example of the imbalance between the private and public sectors of the American economy: "Magnificently efficient factories and oil refineries, a lavish supply of automobiles, a vast consumption of handsomely packaged products, coupled with the absence of a municipal trash collection service which forced the use of home incinerators, made the air nearly unbreathable for an appreciable part of each year." [96]

Bentley's group-conflict theory leaves much to be desired in explaining the kind of social situation Galbraith describes. This is partly because of Bentley's assumption that the end result of the clash of interest groups is a state of balance or equilibrium,[97] and partly because he chooses not to explore the problem of social imbalance generated, at least in part, by ideological forces transcending the arena of group conflict.

Arnold, on the other hand, provides some important insights into the genesis of the imbalance between public and private wealth in contemporary America. He contends that business organizations achieved social dominance by the ingenious ideological tactic of identifying private corporations with the pioneer ethic of the free individual. The American public came to have a strong psychological preference for privately produced goods over services rendered by governmental institutions (pictured as coercive agencies impelled by "politics"). Arnold's observation helps explain why Americans have never taken the pride in the public sector of their society that they have taken in the private sector, and why their accomplishments lie so disproportionately in the private sector.

A second American thinker who joins Arnold in approaching political philosophy and debate in terms of a group struggle is Charles Beard. In his view, the framing and adoption of the Constitution was carried out by a propertied group of men who sought first and foremost to further their own economic interest. The notion that the Constitution was adopted for the "common good" of the "whole people" was simply a rationalization of an underlying economic motive.[98]

Both Beard and Bentley assume that ideology is a dependent variable, arising logically and directly from an underlying group interest. Neither gives proper attention to the possibility that ideology, once generated by group interest, may acquire an independent force of its own, so that it actually shapes social events in a way not directly related to group interests.

Arnold does not overlook this aspect of the complex relationship between groups and ideology. He describes the indignation expressed by a group of bankers, businessmen, lawyers, and professors upon learning that the Interstate Commerce Commission had decreed a drastic reduction of rates for a bankrupt railroad. He notes that none of the men were stockholders of the company, and all would directly benefit from the reduced rates. Their gloom "had its roots not in selfishness nor in the pursuit of the profit of the moment, but in pure idealism." [99] According to Arnold, the ideology or folklore of capitalism grew out of the successful struggle of business groups for social dominance. But in time it became a widely accepted religion whose precepts were often followed in spite of social and personal discomfort.

A comparison of Arnold with Bentley and Beard indicates that he is not the only American thinker who appreciates the insights of seminal European thinkers into the group or class genesis of political philosophy. Arnold's contribution lies in the fact that he applies these insights in a unique way. Unlike Bentley and Beard, Arnold is chiefly interested in the character, content, and impact of ideology as a social force in its own right, and directs his attention to the dominant ideology of post-industrial America.

Arnold has made a second contribution to American thought by dramatically emphasizing, through satire, the facts of the corporate revolution uncovered by the original research efforts of John R. Commons, A. A. Berle, and Gardiner Means.[100]

Commons was one of the first to observe that in the age of large corporations, bargaining transactions (characterized by equality of parties and individual discretion) were increasingly giving way to rationing and managerial transactions (characterized by inequality of parties and the displacement of individual discretion by corporate authority). Arnold dramatized Commons' thesis by poking fun at the folklore which pic-

84

tured corporations as competing individuals in an age when they had assumed the functions of "private governments" and developed the discipline of "armies."

Berle and Means carefully documented the remarkable extent of concentrated corporate power in America. They found in 1930 that two hundred of the nation's 300,000 nonfinancial corporations controlled half of the nation's nonfinancial corporate wealth.[101] They also demonstrated that the most important facet of modern corporate organization was control rather than ownership. The stockholders of large corporations had become too numerous, and their power too dispersed, to retain control of the organizations which they collectively "owned." Management had thus become separated from stock ownership and was a power unto itself.

Arnold added an observational footnote to Berle and Means's findings in his witty account of corporate reorganizations as political struggles for control conducted behind the deceptive symbols of property ownership. Although Arnold provided no new knowledge concerning the corporate revolution, his engaging style succeeded in stimulating thought where the prolix style of John R. Commons or the statistical data of Berle and Means might succeed in inducing drowsiness. Moreover, while others deserve credit for bringing the facts of the corporate revolution to light, Arnold deserves credit for placing these facts in the context of a national ideology which denies them and for grappling with the political problem of reconciling the conflict. Arnold's defense of politics as a reconciling force depending on unifying symbols and ceremonies was a significant contribution to our appreciation of an indispensable profession.

## NOTES

[1] Arnold, "The Folklore of Mr. Hook—A Reply," p. 353.
[2] Ibid., "Law Enforcement—An Attempt at Social Dissection," pp. 3–4.
[3] Ibid., *Folklore of Capitalism*, pp. 350–51.
[4] Ibid., p. 355  [5] pp. 24, 26  [6] p. 136  [7] p. 46.
[8] Ibid., *Symbols of Government*, p. 123.  [9] Ibid. Emphasis mine.
[10] Ibid., *Folklore of Capitalism*, p. 33.  [11] Ibid., p. 84.
[12] Ibid., *Symbols of Government*, p. 229.
[13] Ibid., *Folklore of Capitalism*, p. 378.  [14] Ibid., p. 358  [15] p. 192  [16] p. 150.

[17] Ibid., p. 379   [18] p. 359   [19] p. 380   [20] p. 112.

[21] Ibid., *Symbols of Government*, p. 124.

[22] Ibid., *Folklore of Capitalism*, pp. 107–08.   [23] Ibid., p. 215   [24] p. 185.

[25] Ibid.   [26] Ibid., pp. 185–87   [27] p. 215   [28] p. 216   [29] p. 211   [30] p. 235.

[31] Ibid., p. 237   [32] p. 239   [33] pp. 240–41   [34] p. 263   [35] pp. 264–65.

[36] Ibid., pp. 322–24   [37] pp. 267–68   [38] p. 110   [39] p. 108.

[40] Ibid., *Symbols of Government*, p. 238.   [41] Ibid., p. 240.

[42] Ibid., *Folklore of Capitalism*, p. 205.   [43] Ibid., p. 61   [44] p. 90.

[45] Ibid., p. 92   [46] pp. 6–7   [47] pp. 4–5   [48] pp. 365–66   [49] p. 113.

[50] Ibid., p. 370   [51] p. 115   [52] pp. 37–38   [53] p. 38   [54] pp. 2–3.

[55] Ibid., p. 329   [56] Ibid.   [57] p. 330   [58] p. 331.

[59] Ibid., *Symbols of Government*, p. 114.   [60] Ibid., p. 247   [61] p. 112.

[62] Ibid., *Folklore of Capitalism*, p. 380.

[63] Ibid., *Symbols of Government*, p. 122.   [64] Ibid., p. 235.

[65] Ibid., *Folklore of Capitalism*, p. 138.   [66] Ibid., pp. 343–44.

[67] Ibid., *Symbols of Government*, pp. 251–53.

[68] Ibid., *Folklore of Capitalism*, p. 44.

[69] Ibid., *Symbols of Government*, p. 229.

[70] Ibid., *Folklore of Capitalism*, pp. 161, 162.

[71] Ibid., *Symbols of Government*, pp. 264–65.

[72] Ibid., *Folklore of Capitalism*, p. 391.

[73] Ibid., "The Folklore of Capitalism Revisited," *Yale Review*, vol. 52 (December 1962), p. 193.

[74] Ibid., *Folklore of Capitalism*, p. 334.

[75] Ibid., *Fair Fights and Foul*, pp. 153–55.   [76] Ibid., p. 274.

[77] Ibid., "The Folklore of Capitalism Revisited," p. 202.

[78] Personal interview with Thurman Arnold, October 9, 1966.

[79] Arnold, *Fair Fights and Foul*, pp. 103–04.   [80] Ibid., p. 277.

[81] Ibid., "The Folklore of Capitalism Revisited," p. 198.

[82] Ibid., *Fair Fights and Foul*, p. 80.

[83] Ibid., pp. 279–80. In this description of the "cynical psychiatric attitude" of the American voter in 1960 Arnold provides a strong hint of the source of his own cynicism during the 1930s.

[84] Ibid., pp. 280–81.

[85] Ibid., p. 284. Arnold does not mean by this passage that Lyndon Johnson dealt only in principles, leaving the political manipulation of symbols to lesser men. He believes that all Presidents manipulate symbols for political purposes. His point is that the Goldwater nomination inescapably made the presidential election of 1964 a contest between principles of government whereas the election of 1960 had been more a contest between the personal images projected by the two candidates.

[86] Ibid.   [87] p. 282   [88] p. 285. Emphasis mine.   [89] Ibid.

[90] Sidney Hook, "The Folklore of Capitalism: The Politician's Handbook—a Review," *University of Chicago Law Review*, vol. 5 (April 1938), p. 342.

[91] Arthur F. Bentley, *Process of Government*, pp. 467–68.

[92] R. Joseph Monsen and Mark W. Cannon, *The Makers of Public Policy—American Power Groups and Their Ideologies* (New York: McGraw-Hill, 1965), pp. 24–26.

[93] Bentley, *Process of Government*, pp. 218–20.

94 John Kenneth Galbraith, *The Affluent Society* (Boston: Houghton Mifflin Co., 1958).

95 Ibid., p. 251    96 p. 256.

97 Myron Q. Hale, "The Cosmology of Arthur F. Bentley," *The American Political Science Review,* vol. 54 (December 1960), p. 958.

98 Charles Beard, *Economic Interpretation of the Constitution of the United States,* pp. 16–18.

99 Arnold, *Folklore of Capitalism,* p. 48.

100 John R. Commons, *Institutional Economics* (New York: Macmillan, 1934) and *Legal Foundations of Capitalism* (New York: Macmillan, 1924); Adolf A. Berle and Gardiner Means, *The Modern Corporation and Private Property* (New York: Macmillan, 1933)

101 Berle and Means, *Modern Corporation and Private Property,* p. 28.

# CHAPTER IV

# THE IDEAL OF
# A FREE ECONOMY

In March 1938, the year after *The Folklore of Capitalism* was published, Thurman Arnold was appointed by President Roosevelt as the new head of the Antitrust Division of the Justice Department. The Yale professor who had devised a strategy for politicians in his recent book found himself in a political position of power and importance.

There was more than a little irony in an appointment which placed the author of *The Folklore of Capitalism* in charge of the enforcement of the antitrust laws. In that book, Arnold had described the antitrust laws as "no more than a ceremony of atonement" which had actually protected large combinations by dissipating the energies of reformers in futile efforts. Arnold's remarks in *Folklore* presented him with the formidable task of explaining his present enthusiasm for the antitrust laws to a Senate committee considering the merits of his nomination. He explained to the committee members that his comments in *Folklore* were not attacks on the antitrust laws themselves, but on their ineffective enforcement in the past. "Suppose," said Arnold using a graphic example, "that I would write a book on the pathology of teeth—the cavities, the decay, the various ills that happen to teeth—and then, suppose my critics would say, 'This man is attacking teeth. . . .' " [1] Arnold's examples were persuasive, as indeed they had to be. An influential member of the committee was Senator Borah of whom Arnold had written:"Men like Senator Borah founded political careers on the continuance of such (antitrust) crusades, which were entirely futile but enormously picturesque." [2] When Arnold took his seat before the committee, Senator Borah had a copy of *Folklore* displayed conspicuously before him. Arnold recalls that the senator began reading from the paragraph in which his (Borah's) name appeared and asked the author what he meant. Then Borah skipped the sentences which mentioned his name and read the concluding sentence of the paragraph. "He knew I was worried," Arnold recalled, "and his eyes twinkled. But to my relief, he voted for my confirmation, and thereafter we became friends." [3]

Arnold's discomfort before the Senate committee was part of his adjustment to a new role. As an author, he had been an anthropological observer of social institutions. In 1938, he became a participant in the political drama he had described only a year before. A better understanding of Arnold's philosophy can be gained by an exploration of the relationship between his writings as a detached anthropologist; and his writings, speeches, and actions as an advocate of vigorous antitrust enforcement.

Arnold's basic values did not change when he assumed his new role. In *The Folklore of Capitalism,* he formulated a standard with ideals that could be judged: "For the time being we are adopting the standard that it is a good thing to produce and distribute as much goods as the inventive and organizing genius of man makes possible." [4] The achievement of this goal was Arnold's fundamental objective during his vigorous campaigns to enforce the antitrust laws.

To secure public support for vigorous antitrust enforcement, Arnold became a spirited advocate of a free, competitive economy. This economic ideal had developed in connection with American business organizations and had supported their prestige. Arnold recognized the ideal as a part of America's "vital folklore" and set out to use it for the maximization of production and distribution of goods. This strategy was quite in keeping with Arnold's earlier observation that effective politicians do not try to formulate a new philosophy. Instead, they must select a creed "out of the mass of conflicting ideals which exist in the culture." [5]

Although Arnold's basic purpose and strategy was consistent with his earlier writings, his emphasis shifted as he undertook to enforce the antitrust laws. Before 1938, he envisioned new nonprofit organizations with a new nonprofit creed rising to fill in the gaps left by the older business organizations.[6] After 1938, he asserted that business organizations motivated by the profit creed could best fill in these gaps providing that the antitrust laws were vigorousy enforced.

Arnold was just as willing to use profit-making business organizations and creeds as nonprofit organizations and creeds to attain humanitarian purposes. In 1935, he stated that "the symbols of capitalism are just as adapted to humanitarian distribution of wealth as any others provided we have the will so to use them." [7] This thought seems to have been uppermost in his mind as he earnestly advocated the ideal of a free economy. He described this ideal just as businessmen described it, in terms of a competitive race which fosters private initiative. The most efficient production and distribution of goods, said Arnold, "will come from private initiative in a free market." [8] He described a free market as one in which "every man in America must be free to take a chance, to gamble on his abilities or on the efficiency of his organization, and to win or lose." [9]

Arnold understood that the word "security" had a negative connotation under prevailing beliefs which stressed risk and private initiative. He used this negative symbol to attack private monopolies: "America cannot build a dynamic and expanding economy out of cushions against insecurity. That ideal is the antithesis of the psychological forces which built a dynamic America in the past." [10] The "economics of security," he said, "is based on the assumption that a few men in control of established business institutions must hold control of production and distribution . . . as benevolent trustees for the common good of all." [11]

Ten years after his retirement from the Antitrust Division, Arnold was still espousing competitive slogans. "The economic philosophy behind the antitrust laws," he wrote in 1953, "is a tough philosophy." The laws "recognize that competition means someone may go bankrupt. They do not contemplate the game in which everyone who plays can win." The ideal behind the antitrust laws "remains opportunity for all and security for none." [12] Arnold did not neglect to praise Adam Smith, the great intellectual champion of the competitive ideal: *"The Wealth of Nations* expresses better than any other book the ideal of the antitrust laws. It became the economic bible of the nineteenth century, the greatest period of economic expansion the world had yet known." [13]

Arnold's shift of emphasis in 1938 from nonprofit creeds and institutions to profit creeds and institutions was accompanied by a shift in his concept of the relationship between ideals and institutions. In 1935, Arnold observed that reforms in stable times "are directed only at making an institution conform to its own ideals, an essentially impossible task. . . ." [14] Two years later he asserted that "we who try to make institutions live up to their pretensions are the worst of executives." [15] These statements reflected Arnold's view that ideals can never describe or guide the actual workings of institutions. However, when Arnold became head of the Antitrust Division, he operated under the assumption that business institutions should be required to live up to their own competitive ideals by vigorous enforcement of the antitrust laws.

This view is illustrated by his comments on a brochure issued by a large oil company praising the competitive ideal. One caption read: "Man Never Runs as Fast Against Time as in a Race." The conclusion was, "Competition is the one incentive discovered so far that keeps him constantly striving to improve his products and lower his costs." [16] Arnold noted that the very oil company which issued the pamphlet had attempted to keep competing producers out of the market by refusing to sell its products to any filling station which carried the products of a competing company. Arnold considered this a good example of "our present confusion between our economic ideals and our business practice. . . . Never in our history has so much been said in praise of free competitive enterprise. Yet never in our history has there been a greater concentration of economic power in a few hands." [17] As head of the Antitrust Division, Arnold was not content to accept disparity between business ideals and practice as an inevitable fact of life. He realized that competitive ideals could never be fully realized in practice, but he was sincere in his attempt to make them as much a reality as possible.

Although Arnold took competitive slogans seriously as guides for business practice, he was also aware of their powerful force as symbols and used them simultaneously as devices to be manipulated for purposes of public acceptance and as tools for achieving practical economic results. Arnold did not forget his observation in 1937 that an effective creed must be based on a simple and understandable ideal capable of personification.[18] He repeatedly used the figure of Henry Ford to illustrate the competitive ideal and to support his campaign against monopoly. When businessmen accused Arnold of promoting cutthroat competition and attacking profits, he answered that he was doing nothing more than maintaining conditions under which nonconformists like Henry Ford, who was considered a menace by the leading automobile manufacturers of his day, could freely enter the market. It is true, said Arnold, that Ford disrupted the automobile industry by mass production and price cutting. But it was because of the competitive struggle which Ford initiated that inexpensive automobiles were made available to the average consumer.[19]

Arnold's appreciation of the importance of symbols in gaining public acceptance was manifest in his use of colorful language and dramatic tactics to strengthen the enforcement of the antitrust laws. He described the responsibilities of the Antitrust Division as being similar to the duties of a traffic policeman. "The maintenance of a free market," he said, "is as much a matter of constant policing as is the flow of free traffic on a busy intersection." [20] He pictured private restraints of trade as exorbitant toll charges: "A number of new economic toll bridges are being erected at various stages of the distribution process . . . they are based upon deliberate agreements in restraint of trade, entered into with a view to what the traffic will bear." [21] On other occasions, he spoke of private monopoly as "an economic disease which is endemic in all commercial civilization—the disease of cartelization, or the hardening of the arteries of commerce." [22]

Arnold utilized grand jury investigations and criminal indictments in such a way as to achieve a dramatic as well as a practical effect. He would choose a certain industry in which practices in restraint of trade were flagrant, and launch a massive investigation of all the distribution points between the producer and the consumer. Such a show of activity, contended Arnold, "causes businessmen and consumers who have been the victims of improper practices to take heart and offer their active cooperation." [23] He was well aware, as he had been in his earlier writings, of the importance of drama in building morale. "It takes the shock of indictments," he observed, "to clean up a bad situation in the distribution of a product. But after that shock is over, it takes only slight supervision to keep the market free." [24] As one student of Arnold's antitrust program concluded: "Arnold set out to dramatize the issues, 'manipulate the symbols,' and enlist popular support. His use of public statements, criminal indictments, and mass investigations was part of the dramatizing process. The appeal to the revered traditions of the Sherman Act was another part. The colorful language in which he outlined his program was still another." [25]

The most important symbol in Arnold's campaign to enlist popular support was the Sherman Antitrust Act and the competitive tradition which it represented. Although writing as an advocate in 1940, Arnold reiterated many of his earlier anthropological observations in the process of recommending the Sherman Act as a tool for economic regulation. Social institutions, he observed, are like human personalities, responding to pressure rather than to logical thinking. Adjustment to these pressures is made easier and less painful by avoiding methods which attack traditional ideals.[26] New governmental programs which depart from tradition face a long spiritual struggle which prevents their efficient administration for years. For this reason: "A new idea must appear to be an old idea before it will work at all . . . the easiest remedies for democracy to apply are those which do not depart too far from tradition." [27] The strength of the Sherman Act, concluded Arnold, is that it "is a symbol of our traditional ideals." [28]

The Sherman Act had the additional advantage of being associated in the public mind with the revered judicial process. In 1935, Arnold had distinguished between the "spiritual government" of the courts, representing the ideal of law above government, and the "temporal government" of the administrative agencies, representing the ideal of governmental regulation of business.[29] The latter, he contended, were struggling for acceptance in an atmosphere which accorded the greatest prestige and honor to the courts. When Arnold became head of the Antitrust Division three years later, he took pains to associate his activities with the spiritual government of the courts and to dissociate his organization from the image of an administrative agency. Many reformers, he observed, preferred "a shiny new administrative machine" to the judicial process which appeared "clumsy and covered with barnacles. . . ." However, the public's deep distrust of administrative tribunals renders them ineffective instruments of economic regulation.[30]

93

Arnold's strategy was to use revered judicial symbols, which he had earlier associated with "spiritual" *resistance* to economic regulation, for the purpose of gaining *acceptance* for such regulation. He described the Antitrust Division as standing with the courts above political pressures. "Legislative measures," he said, "are too close to pressure groups immediately affected to perform the necessary function of breaking up capitalized restraints of trade." [31] "This makes it all the more essential that the organization which attacks the bottlenecks of business be removed from these political pressures or its efforts will fail." [32]

Arnold's alliance with the "spiritual government" of the courts resulted in some important legal victories. He succeeded in bringing the medical profession within the scope of the antitrust laws.[33] He initiated a successful antitrust suit against monopolistic practices in the motion picture industry.[34] He successfully attacked a local monopoly in the dairy industry by establishing that it was not exempted from the antitrust laws by the Agricultural Adjustment Act.[35] By continuing a suit initiated by his predecessor, Robert Jackson, he obtained a Supreme Court ruling that patents could not be used by the patentee to dominate resale prices and methods of marketing products after the patentee had sold them.[36] Perhaps Arnold's most dramatic achievement was the host of indictments he obtained during a nationwide investigation of the building and construction industries.

Arnold was a very important "middle man" in the government's famous antitrust battle with the Aluminum Company of America (better known as Alcoa). He inherited the case from Robert Jackson and kept the legal battle going for some three years. His contention that Alcoa was a monopoly in restraint of trade was rejected in 1941 by a New York district court.[37] After Arnold retired, Solicitor General Fahy succeeded in obtaining an important reversal of the district court's decision. The Second Circuit Court of Appeals held, in 1945, that the acquisition of monopolistic power per se was illegal, even where there was no act of aggression against existing competitors. The fact that a business practice placed *potential* competitors at an overwhelming disadvantage was sufficient to make the practice illegal.[38] One of the many charges made in Arnold's unsuccessful suit in the district court clearly anticipated the 1945 ruling. The government contended that Alcoa's complete monopoly over the production and sale of "virgin aluminum" in the United States put potential competitors "at the mercy of a single powerful corporation controlling essential raw materials." This arrangement had the direct effect of "suppressing and preventing substantial competition which would otherwise arise." [39]

Ten years after his retirement from the Antitrust Division, Arnold was still defending the Sherman Act with a "spiritual" appeal remarkably similar to the conservative arguments he had satirized before 1938. In *The Folklore of Capitalism,* for example, he humorously described the invocation of elevated principles, usually associated with the Constitution, to defend existing economic arrangements. He satirized the tendency to invent a future economic Hell, frequently associated with alien political systems, as a punishment for deserting those principles.[40] In 1953, however, he was ardently defending the antitrust laws as "our economic constitution, our charter of commercial freedom." Because the courts of justice have enforced this charter, he contended, American business institutions have not followed the noncompetitive path of business institutions in Western Europe.[41] Arnold warned Americans that they could not safely abandon the principles of the Sherman Act: "The permanent abandonment of our economic constitution represented by the Sherman Act would have had incalculable consequences for free enterprise in our economic future." [42] The present danger, concluded Arnold, is that "we are frightened of economic freedom and too ready to exchange our birthright for a ration of security." [43]

Arnold's rhetoric linked the Sherman Act, not only with judicial institutions, but also with the cherished ideals of freedom and democracy: "The only type of economic structure in which government is free and in which the human spirit is free is one in which commerce is free. . . . The suppression of democratic freedom always follows the suppression of the free exchange of goods. . . ." [44] Arnold observed that commercial civilizations which have allowed experimentation in industry and production have also encouraged new experiments in art and literature. "Free commercial enterprise," he concluded, "breeds free dissemination of ideas. Freedom from intellectual tyranny is impossible without freedom from commercial tyranny." [45]

The great threat to "industrial democracy," according to Arnold, is the private seizure of economic power by secret means. Public grants of economic power are made in the open by democratic processes, and can be terminated by those processes. Private seizure of industrial power, however, is "veiled in the mystery of meetings and boards of direc-

95

tors. . . ." Such power is not subject to public debate or to periodic elections and recognizes no public responsibility.[46] Arnold was convinced that opposition to the private seizure of economic power by *sub rosa* agreements was a widely shared sentiment which gave ideological impetus to the Sherman Act:

"It is the fact that the Sherman Act bars the way to private seizure of industrial power that gives it its continuing force and its constant public acceptance." [47]

Arnold used the positive symbol of "industrial democracy" in contrast to the negative symbol of "socialism" to gain public support for antitrust enforcement. He contended that when private parties are allowed to build industrial empires in violation of the competitive ideal, socialism eventually follows. This is because prices set by private agreements rather than by competitive forces lose touch with consumer purchasing power, and the government is forced to take control to avert economic chaos.[48] Arnold was employing familiar rhetoric in arguing that private monopolies would lead America down the road to socialism. He described his antitrust program as a safeguard against that grim future.

The adept use of competitive symbols was the first distinctive characteristic of Arnold's antitrust campaign. The second was his emphasis on practical economic results. Arnold's program combined the symbolic and the practical in an effort to use revered economic slogans to obtain tangible economic benefits for the consumer. He recently compared Franklin Roosevelt's antitrust policies, with which he was identified, to those of Theodore Roosevelt. The comparison illustrates his appreciation of both the symbolic and practical aspects of the antitrust laws. Arnold contended that Theodore Roosevelt never used the Sherman Act as a practical instrument. His achievement "was to enshrine the ideal of the act as a part of our national folklore." He made the policy of the Sherman Act "an economic religion and its violation an economic sin. . . ." Although he did not prevent large concentrations of economic power, he did prevent such concentrations from gaining a legitimate place in our national values.[49] Franklin Roosevelt proved to be a more effective trustbuster than Theodore Roosevelt. He treated the antitrust laws as a practical instrument for maintaining competition across the nation.[50]

During his first year as head of the Antitrust Division, Arnold delivered a speech in which he colorfully described his strategy for bringing the economic ideals of America into peaceful coexistence with its practical needs: "We must first make obeisance to the ideals, the mystery, the romance and magic which give our social organizations the flavor and character which we revere and then emerge from the church to the back-yard where wood needs to be sawed." [51]

Arnold explained that by "sawing wood" he meant the full utilization of productive capacity. This could be achieved by adjusting prices to income. "My hope is," he said, "that the adjustment between prices and incomes may be made within the limits of our competitive ideal of free and independent producers, buyers, and sellers." [52] In another address, Arnold spoke again about the practical economic problem of unused capacity and its relation to the consumer. He cited a Brookings Institution study which estimated that over a ten-year period America could have produced $248 billion more of goods and services had its productive facilities been used to full capacity. Consumer-minded Arnold did not neglect to point out that this would have amounted to $8,000 per family over the ten-year period.[53]

Arnold was determined to transform the antitrust laws from mere preaching devices to practical tools for improving production and distribution. The only sensible way to apply the antitrust laws to an industrial combination, he thought, was to determine whether the combination increases the efficiency of production or distribution and passes the savings on to the consumer. Businesses should not be attacked simply because they are large. If they can demonstrate that their great size contributes to the efficiency of mass production and distribution, they do not violate the purpose of the antitrust laws.[54]

Arnold's strategy for obtaining practical economic results was to concentrate on one industry at a time. He chose industries of practical importance to the consumer where there was strong evidence of practices impeding the efficient distribution of a product. Once an industry was chosen, Arnold's plan was to ". . . investigate every step from the raw material to the consumer, and prosecute simultaneously restraints which put an artificial obstacle on the distribution of that product." [55] The purpose of Arnold's strategy was to remove the Sherman Act from the realm of abstract law and make it a highly visible protector of the consumer's pocketbook.

Arnold had been convinced before 1938 that no practical results could be achieved without an effective organization. He observed in *The Folklore of Capitalism* that antitrust campaigns were "well supplied with

97

orators and economists, but . . . lacked practical organizers." [56] Arnold's hope that the antitrust laws might be forged into a practical tool rested on his determination to back his program with an effective organization: "The question arises whether this is just another sporadic crusade like those of the past, or whether it is the beginning of a nationwide organization which is actually adequate to protect the interests of the consumer." [57]

Arnold noted that during the famous trust-busting crusade of Theodore Roosevelt, the personnel of the Antitrust Division consisted of five lawyers and four stenographers.[58] Arnold insisted that he needed more funds and personnel to organize antitrust proceedings into purposive programs capable of bringing economic results, and he was successful in obtaining both. During his five years as head of the Antitrust Division, appropriations rose from about $473,000 to $1.8 million, and personnel increased from 111 to 496.[59] Part of Arnold's efforts to build an effective organization consisted of training new personnel in practical techniques: "New staff members were subjected to intensive instruction in psychological devices, business structures, grand jury investigations, and the proper methods of building a case." [60] These efforts resulted in a competent and effective organization with high morale and a new sense of purpose.

Arnold relied on the consumer consciousness of the American people to provide grass-roots support for his organization. He felt that consumers were becoming increasingly aware that unregulated business institutions could not satisfactorily distribute goods and provide jobs. He was convinced that the consumer movement had become strong enough to support an adequate antitrust enforcement organization.[61]

Despite his effectiveness as an organizer, Arnold's program fell short of the practical achievements he had hoped for. With the coming of World War II, the arguments for economic controls and a planned economy gained momentum. Arnold replied with arguments for vigorous enforcement of the antitrust laws couched in the slogans of national defense: "Industrial democracy . . . can defend itself. It is only economic feudalism masquerading under the name of democracy that is unable to unite to serve a common national end." [62] Despite Arnold's arguments, influence within the Roosevelt Administration shifted from the antimonopolists to the business-oriented directors of the new defense agencies.

The antitrust program lost momentum as more and more concessions had to be made in the name of national defense.[63]

Arnold's program had other practical difficulties in addition to those caused by the war. His emphasis on the courts and the maintenance of tradition meant, in practice, an emphasis on litigation rather than economic reconstruction. The Antitrust Division frequently had trouble translating its legal victories into economic results.[64] Moreover, the potent consumer movement on which Arnold relied for grass-roots support did not materialize. Americans, for the most part, tended to remain producer conscious. The immediate interests of many Americans as producers outweighed their less immediate interests as consumers.[65] This was especially true because Arnold was attacking not only restraints of trade by business but also by labor unions.

Because of the practical difficulties that confronted Arnold's program, it achieved only limited economic results. It accomplished a number of localized changes but failed to bring an overall economic recovery. This is not to say that Arnold's efforts were in vain. His vigorous investigation and prosecution policies succeeded in making businessmen more cautious about what they attempted. Moreover, his imaginative program paved the way for a broader interpretation of the antitrust laws after the war.[66]

Perhaps the practical limitations of Arnold's program are partially explainable in terms of Arnold's own analysis of the political process in his writings before 1938. He observed that political institutions rarely move in a single, logically consistent direction. Rather, they move in different and frequently contradictory directions at the same time to reconcile conflicting ideals within society. The New Deal was a perfect example of this process, and the early New Deal marched to the tune of the National Recovery Act. This legislation, as Arnold observed, represented many different ideals. Its dominant ideal, however, was economic planning, and its practical effect was to fortify private monopolistic arrangements.[67] When Arnold launched his antitrust program in 1938, he found himself faced with monopolies that had been fortified by earlier New Deal programs.

The conflicting ideals within the New Deal reflected the attitudes of the public at large. Americans desired a high standard of living, which necessitated a high degree of planned industrial organization; at the same time, they wished to preserve the individualistic ideal of competition and protection of the "little fellow." These two inconsistent ideals were so intermixed in the philosophy of the average man that any administration wishing to retain power had to make concessions to both of them. For this delicate political task, Franklin Roosevelt was ideally suited: "His mixed emotions so closely reflected the popular mind that they were a political asset rather than a liability." [68]

The revival of the antitrust laws in 1938 represented a change of emphasis from economic planning to regulated competition. Yet so deeply ingrained were both of these approaches in the ideology of the New Deal that it is doubtful if one could ever have entirely displaced the other.[69] Franklin Roosevelt, more than Arnold himself, resembled Arnold's earlier description of the "humanitarian politician" opportunistically trying to obtain economic results within a context of conflicting ideals. Roosevelt initially responded to economic distress by emphasizing the ideal of planning. With the failure of the National Recovery Act and the recession of 1937, his emphasis shifted to the competitive ideal of the antitrust laws. As the Second World War approached, he moved back toward the ideal of planning.

The distinctive characteristic of Arnold's approach, with its successes and failures, was the utilization of competitive symbols to obtain practical economic results. Persons familiar with Arnold's earlier writings may have expected him to become something of a cynical manipulator viewing the competitive ideal as hokum to be opportunistically exploited. However, once Arnold had shaped the ideal of a free economy into a force for practical action, he came to believe in it, not as a cynical manipulator, but as a sincere and ardent advocate. As a recent student of Arnold's career has concluded: "In spite of all his nonconformity . . . and in spite of his sly ridicule of the capitalist system, Arnold was apparently an intense believer in a competitive economy and in the idea that such an economy had never had a real chance." [70]

After his resignation from the Antitrust Division in 1943, Arnold continued his ardent advocacy of the ideal of a free economy in his new judicial position of associate justice on the Circuit Court of Appeals for the District of Columbia. In *The Folklore of Capitalism* and in his statements as head of the Antitrust Division, Arnold had called attention to the use of the patent privilege by large corporations to gain monopolistic control of various markets. Perhaps his most distinctive contribution as judge on the Court of Appeals was a series of opinions in which he assailed the use of the patent laws for monopolistic purposes.[71]

Speaking for the court in *Potts* v. *Coe*, Judge Arnold in a joint opinion with Judge Miller, held that gradual advances in scientific knowledge made possible by the funds and research organizations of large corporations could not be considered an "invention" within the meaning of the patent laws. Patents, he said, are intended as rewards for inventive genius on the part of an individual, not "as a reward for the collective achievement of a corporate research organization." Judge Arnold noted that in the present case, an expert employee had been required to assign in advance all his future patent rights to the Teletype Corporation. Such an arrangement, he observed, "reflects the respective contributions of the organization and the individual to these so-called inventions." To give patents for such routine experimentation by large organizations, concluded Arnold, is to use the patent law to create corporate monopolies rather than to reward men of inventive genius.[72]

Seven months later, the court considered a motion to vacate its decision in the *Potts* case. Judge Arnold wrote a second opinion for the court in which he stated more fully the ideal of a free economy as applied to technological discovery: "The patent law is designed to encourage competition among inventors by giving a patent to the ingenious individual who wins in a race for discovery. The modern corporate research laboratory is a negation of this principle because it is compelled to suppress competition between individuals." [73]

A court which ignores this fact when applying the patent law, said Judge Arnold, is "promoting a fiction which inevitably leads to the monopoly grants to corporations on the technical education of our time." Judge Arnold's comment brings to mind his earlier observations concerning the "personification of the corporation." In *The Folklore of Capitalism*, he described the many ways in which corporate power was legitimized by the fiction that corporations were individuals and thus entitled to the rights and privileges of individuals. His judicial opinions in the *Potts* case were clearly intended to prevent this fiction from influencing the operation of the patent law.

Arnold continued to be a strong advocate of the ideal of a free economy after he terminated his brief judicial career in July 1945 to return to a private law practice. Perhaps his most fervent defense of the Sherman Act appeared in the *Atlantic Monthly* in 1953.[74] This inspirational article, written eight years after Arnold had left the political and judicial stage, and aimed at a sophisticated audience, suggests the sincerity of his belief in the competitive ideal. Seven years later, he was still defending the Sherman Act as "The Law to Make Free Enterprise Free." [75]

From 1938 to 1943, Arnold made a bold and vigorous attempt to bring the antitrust laws abreast of modern economic conditions. His antitrust philosophy had the avowed purpose of serving consumers by making more goods available at lower prices. He operated on the assumption that a nationwide restoration of competition would cure most of the economic ills of the Depression.

The purely economic achievements of the antitrust laws since Arnold's departure from the Antitrust Division in 1943 have fallen far short of his optimistic expectations. One reason for this may be that Arnold overestimated the extent to which monopolistic practices reduced the living standards of Americans. A study published in 1954 by Arnold Harberger concludes that the elimination of resource misallocation resulting from monopolistic practices in American manufacturing during the late 1920s would have brought with it an improvement in consumer welfare of just a little more than a tenth of one percent or, in present values, about $2 per capita.[76] David Schwartzman similarly concluded, on the basis of a study of Canadian and American manufacturing firms, that the misallocation of funds by way of "monopoly profits" had been overestimated.[77] Another scholar interested in the antitrust laws draws the broader conclusion that "if economic tests alone are applied there is little reason to believe that 75 years of antitrust have done the country more good than ill." [78] Some observers go even further by charging that recent applications of the antitrust laws by the courts and enforcement agencies have sacrificed the consumer's interest in productive efficiency to protect smaller, less efficient firms which cannot benefit from the economies of large-scale operations.[79]

Recent studies and observations by specialists concerned with antitrust cast considerable doubt on Arnold's central trust-busting rationale, i.e., that vigorous enforcement of the antitrust laws would result in a dramatic increase in production and a significant improvement in living standards.

Contemporary students of antitrust are more inclined to emphasize the social and political impact of the antitrust laws than their effect on economic performance. Blake and Jones, for example, defend the antitrust laws by contending "that economic efficiency, in terms of short-run adjustments, may on occasion be less important to public policy than the diffusion and control of economic power." [80] Without this diffusion of power, the authors conclude, bureaucratic control or public ownership would become necessary.

There is a consensus among economists that repeal of the antitrust laws would result in much greater size and concentration of American industrial firms which, in turn, would increase political pressures to bring them under public control. Donald Dewey concludes that "While antitrust may be largely irrelevant to the economic performance of the American economy, it may be absolutely indispensable to the political survival of American capitalism." [81]

This contemporary observation indicates that Arnold's most important contribution to our understanding of the role of the antitrust laws is probably to be found in *The Folklore of Capitalism* where he describes the antitrust laws as *symbols of legitimacy* for business institutions. In Western European nations, where there is no strong antitrust tradition, business firms employ other symbols of legitimacy, e.g., the representation of trade unions on boards of directors in Germany. Arnold's witty observations in *Folklore* contain the important insight that, in America, the antitrust laws are not "antibusiness," but actually make industrial power legitimate by bringing it within the concept of free competition. Arnold was incorrect, however, to imply (before becoming a trustbuster) that the antitrust laws had only a symbolic significance. On the contrary, they are the major reason why a cartel system, like those found in Western Europe, has not developed in America. Although the antitrust laws have not influenced economic performance to the extent that trustbuster Arnold thought possible, they have affected economic structure to a greater extent than satirist Arnold led his readers to expect in *The Folklore of Capitalism*.

Arnold's trust-busting campaigns were based on the assumption that a nationwide restoration of competition would create a more prosperous society by closing the gap between actual and potential industrial production. Restoration of competition, however, did not turn out to be the decisive factor in eliminating the vast unused industrial capacity which characterized the Depression. Rather, the approach of the Second World War and the rapid development of war industries proved to be decisive.

The onset of a protracted "cold war" after the defeat of Germany seemed to ensure that the major responsibility for promoting the full use of industrial capacity would be filled, not by a restoration of competition but by a thriving war industry operating largely under government direction.[82]

Even if international tensions are somehow reduced, it seems likely that policymakers will continue to prefer direct or indirect public planning as a means of ensuring full production. As Robert Heilbroner has pointed out, modern technology has created social problems which require *nonmarket* controls to forestall.[83] Antitrust programs, no matter how vigorous, cannot deal with these problems. Therefore, the postwar pattern of filling in economic gaps by public funds and public direction is likely to be continued. In the last several years, Arnold himself seemed to have accepted this conclusion. While voicing his respect for antitrust laws and the competitive tradition, he placed his greatest emphasis on the need for increased public spending for badly needed social services.[84]

Arnold's writings on antitrust after 1938, although not likely to be remembered as contributions to American social and economic thought, give valuable insights into his most enduring commitments. They reveal, for example, that he was a sincere idealist, far less cynical than the manipulator whose praises he sang in his earlier writings. Once Arnold had shaped the ideal of a free economy into a rationale for practical humanitarian action, he proceeded to ignore his former assertion that ideals should never guide institutions. In his early writings, Arnold contended that practical institutions needed to escape from their ideals to be effective. As head of the Antitrust Division, he asserted that business institutions could not be effective if they were allowed to escape from their competitive ideals.

The constant current which flows through Arnold's writings before and after 1938 was his stress on the use of accepted ideals to achieve humanitarian economic goals. The changes in his approach after 1938 indicate that the material well-being of all Americans was far more important in his thinking than maintaining a consistent intellectual position concerning the relationship between social ideals and institutions.

## NOTES

[1] Edwards, "Thurman Arnold and the Antitrust Laws," p. 339.

[2] Arnold, *Folklore of Capitalism*, p. 217.

[3] Ibid., *Fair Fights and Foul*, p. 137.

[4] Ibid., *Folklore of Capitalism*, p. 177.  [5] Ibid., pp. 161–62  [6] p. 347.

[7] Ibid., *Symbols of Government*, p. 235.

[8] Ibid., *Democracy and Free Enterprise* (Norman: University of Oklahoma Press, 1942), p. 46.

[9] Ibid., *Cartels or Free Enterprise?* Public Affairs Pamphlet No. 103 (New York: Public Affairs Committee, 1945), p. 4.

[10] Ibid., p. 27  [11] p. 4.

[12] Ibid., "The Sherman Act on Trial," *Atlantic Monthly*, vol. 192 (July 1953), p. 38.  [13] Ibid., p. 40.

[14] Ibid., *Symbols of Government*, p. 124.

[15] Ibid., *Folklore of Capitalism*, p. 378.

[16] Ibid., *Cartels or Free Enterprise?*, p. 1.  [17] Ibid., pp. 5–7.

[18] Ibid., *Folklore of Capitalism*, p. 139.

[19] Ibid., *The Bottlenecks of Business* (New York: Reynal & Hitchcock, 1940), pp. 119–21.  [20] Ibid., p. 122  [21] p. 219.

[22] Ibid., *Democracy and Free Enterprise*, p. 30.

[23] Ibid., *Bottlenecks of Business*, p. 201.  [24] Ibid., p. 204.

[25] Ellis W. Hawley, *The New Deal and the Problem of Monopoly* (Princeton, N.J.: Princeton University Press, 1966), p. 431.

[26] Arnold, *Bottlenecks of Business*, p. 92.  [27] Ibid., p. 96  [28] p. 92.

[29] Ibid., *Symbols of Government*, pp. 127, 194.

[30] Ibid., *Bottlenecks of Business*, pp. 99–100.  [31] Ibid., p. 291  [32] p. 289.

[33] *United States* v. *American Medical Association*. 28 F. Supp. 752 (1939).

[34] *United States* v. *Paramount Pictures*. 70 F. Supp. 53 (1947); 334 U.S. 131 (1948).

[35] *United States* v. *Borden Co. et al.* 308 U.S. 188 (1939).

[36] *United States* v. *Ethyl Gasoline Corp.* 309 U.S. 436 (1940).

[37] *United States* v. *Aluminum Co. of America*. 44 F. Supp. 97 (1941).

[38] *United States* v. *Aluminum Co. of America*. 148 F. 2d, 416, 431 (1945). Alcoa had expanded its productive capacity to meet all anticipated future demand when it was already the sole supplier of aluminum in the United States.

[39] *United States* v. *Aluminum Co. of America*. 44 F. Supp. 97, 150–51 (1941).

[40] Arnold, *Folklore of Capitalism*, pp. 4–5, 14–15.

[41] Ibid., "The Sherman Act on Trial," p. 39.  [42] Ibid.  [43] p. 40.

[44] Ibid., *Bottlenecks of Business*, p. 283.

[45] Ibid.  [46] p. 110  [47] p. 97  [48] p. 112.

[49] Ibid., *Fair Fights and Foul*, p. 128.  [50] Ibid., p. 139.

[51] Edwards, "Thurman Arnold and the Antitrust Laws," p. 340.  [52] Ibid.

[53] Thurman Arnold, "Free Trade Within the Borders of the United States," *South Carolina Bar Association: Transactions of the 47th Annual Meeting*, April 1940, p. 94.

[54] Ibid., *Bottlenecks of Business,* p. 125.

[55] Ibid., "Free Trade Within the Borders of the United States," p. 97.

[56] Ibid., *Folklore of Capitalism,* p. 220.

[57] Ibid., *Bottlenecks of Business,* p. 282.   [58] Ibid., pp. 170–71.

[59] Edwards, "Thurman Arnold and the Antitrust Laws," p. 339.

[60] Hawley, *New Deal and Problem of Monopoly,* p. 432.

[61] Arnold, *Bottlenecks of Business,* pp. 261, 281.   [62] Ibid., p. 78.

[63] Hawley, *New Deal and Monopoly,* p. 442.

[64] Ibid., p. 450. See also Walton H. Hamilton and Irene Till, "Antitrust—the Reach after New Weapons," *Washington University Law Quarterly,* vol. 26 (December 1940), pp. 1, 7.

[65] Hawley, *New Deal and Monopoly,* p. 447.   [66] Ibid., p. 454   [67] p. 479.

[68] Ibid., pp. 475–76   [69] pp. 489–90   [70] p. 423.

[71] *Potts* v. *Coe,* 78 U.S. App. D.C. 297, Decided Jan. 18, 1944; *Special Equipment Co.* v. *Coe,* 79 U.S. App. D.C. 133, Decided June 19, 1944; *Monsanto Chemical Co.* v. *Coe,* 79 U.S. App. D.C. 155, Decided June 26, 1944; *Potts* v. *Coe,* 79 U.S. App. D.C. 223, Decided August 7, 1944.

[72] *Potts* v. *Coe.* 78 U.S. App. D.C. 297, at 301.

[73] *Potts* v. *Coe.* 79 U.S. App. D.C. 223, at 227.

[74] Arnold, "The Sherman Act on Trial," pp. 38–42.

[75] Ibid., "The Law to Make Free Enterprise Free," *American Heritage,* vol. 11 (October 1960), pp. 52–55, 92–94.

[76] Arnold C. Harberger, "Monopoly and Resource Allocation," *American Economic Review,* vol. 44 (May 1954), p. 84.

[77] David Schwartzman, "The Effect of Monopoly on Price," *Journal of Political Economy,* vol. 67 (August 1959), pp. 360–61.

[78] Donald Dewey, "The Shaky Case for Antitrust," *Challenge,* vol. 14 (January/February 1966), p. 19.

[79] Robert H. Bork and Ward S. Bowman, "The Crisis in Antitrust," *Columbia Law Review,* vol. 65 (March 1965), pp. 363–76.

[80] Harlan M. Blake and William K. Jones, "In Defense of Antitrust," *Columbia Law Review,* vol. 65 (March 1965), p. 381.

[81] Dewey, "The Shaky Case for Antitrust," p. 43.

[82] See John Kenneth Galbraith, *The New Industrial State* (Boston: Houghton Mifflin Co., 1967).

[83] Robert L. Heilbroner, *The Limits of American Capitalism* (New York: Harper & Row, 1965), p. 118.

[84] See Arnold, *Fair Fights and Foul.*

CHAPTER V

# THE IDEAL OF THE LAW

According to Arnold, legal ideals, like other ideals, do not describe or guide the actual workings of the institutions which produce them. Their function is rather that of maintaining the morale of persons closely connected with those institutions or in some way identified with them. Legal ideals maintain morale in four important ways: by conferring prestige on judicial institutions, by producing a feeling of unity and comfort in society, by creating an atmosphere of tolerance, and by dramatizing humanitarian values.

The prestige enjoyed by judicial institutions is based on the ideal of supremacy of law as applied by impartial judges. Although most judges are elected, they are viewed as the most trustworthy protectors of society from the tyranny of the majority.[1] Judges are different from bureaucrats and Congressmen in that they are guided by reason rather than by personal preference. This impartiality is society's guarantee of the rule of law above the whims of men. "It is obvious," said Arnold, "that our belief that courts are the chief guardians of the supremacy of law is the reason why we adopt such a respectful attitude toward them." [2]

The ideal of legal supremacy is manifested by reverence for the Constitution. This document became, like the Bible, an object of popular worship. Most of those who revered and worshiped the Constitution ". . . knew approximately as much about the history and dialectic of that document as the masses in the Middle Ages knew about the Bible —in those days when people were not permitted to read the Bible." [3] Men might be permitted to choose between sound and unsound economic theory, but they could not be permitted to choose between sound and unsound constitutional theory. "To prevent them from erring on this point," Arnold observed, "a scholargarchy was set up, with complete autocratic power." [4] In this fashion, constitutionalism was translated into judicial prestige and power.

Arnold contended that the ideal of constitutionalism has a habit of appearing even where there is no constitution. In 1921, he observed, the revolutionary courts of Russia were opposed to the new economic policy of Lenin. They gained moral support from the only Russian legal periodical of the time which warned of the "danger of being drowned by the petty bourgeois wave" and urged the courts to "preserve their own proletarian essence." [5] Such legal utterances in a nation whose ideological structure is so different from America's indicated to Arnold that judicial institutions develop common patterns of thought regardless of their origin: "Just as a ship gathers barnacles or an oyster secretes pearls (the choice of the figure depending on one's attitude) so does a judicial institution accumulate great defensive fundamental principles." [6]

Arnold describes the way in which, during the New Deal period, courts combined the ideal of legal supremacy with shrewd judicial strategy to preserve their supremacy over expanding regulatory bodies. When the first epoch-making acts of the New Deal were passed, the Supreme Court was silent. During the period of public enthusiasm over these new policies, the court consistently avoided comment on their constitutionality.[7] By virtue of this brooding silence, Arnold noted that the court "hung like an ominous cloud over those who were attempting new forms of control." [8] New regulations were enforced half-heartedly out of fear that a future decision might declare them void from the beginning.[9] Finally, when the public had become disillusioned with the recovery legislation, the court declared it unconstitutional in *Schechter Poultry Corp.*

v. *United States*.[10] In making its decision, however, the court left no certain way of telling whether other acts pending before Congess (e.g., the Social Security bill and the Wagner Labor bill) were constitutional.[11] The court's power to create "a cloud of hampering uncertainty" over the activities of new regulatory bodies gave it a great strategic advantage in its efforts to maintain judicial supremacy.

The strategic position of the judicial system, Arnold contended, rested mainly on the legal notion of "trial by combat." According to this notion, courts stand aloof from regulation, confining their efforts to settling contests between parties. Each battle is viewed as a war to end wars, because it will give rise to legal principles which will make future contests unnecessary.[12] By limiting themselves to deciding only contests between parties, the courts could escape passing on regulations at unpropitious times; or, they could "take pot shots at specific regulations without ever being forced to assume responsibility for the regulatory scheme as a whole." [13] In other words, the courts were able to maintain "great supervisory power with a minimum of executive responsibility." [14] Arnold concluded that the notion of trial by combat, rather than any particular constitutional decision, was the force that kept the conservative tradition alive during the early New Deal period.[15]

By combining the ideal of legal supremacy with astute judicial strategy, the courts were able to maintain a spiritual hierarchy which reinforced their own power and prestige. At the top of this hierarchy were the courts, bound by fundamental law. At the bottom were the bureaus, bound by red tape rather than law. Between the bureaus and the courts were the commissions with quasi-judicial powers. While these bodies were not exactly courts, they were more like courts than like bureaus.[16]

During the 1930s, Arnold's main concern had been to give greater freedom of action to the government bureaus attempting new forms of economic regulation. He suggested ways to loosen the stranglehold of the judiciary over administrative tribunals.[17] In later years, he saw the government bureaus grow in power, and their relationship to the "spiritual government" of the courts undergo a fundamental change. In 1962, he wrote, "Our courts, which before the great depression were accustomed to review decisions of administrative tribunals with meticulous care, now affirm them if there is the slightest supporting evidence." [18]

Administrative tribunals, Arnold maintained, are immunized from judicial review by the doctrine that they are composed of experts in their particular fields, whereas the courts lack such expertise. The situation that Arnold described in 1962 seems to be almost the reverse of that described in 1935. In *The Symbols of Government,* he spoke of administrative tribunals, who based their decisions on expertise rather than on symbols, being demoralized and hampered by judicial review.

As the relationship between the courts and the regulatory bureaucracy changed, Arnold's emphasis also changed from stress on freedom of action and experimentation for the bureaucracy to protection of individual liberty from bureaucratic encroachment. Arnold recently observed that, under the cloak of deference to expertise, "Many of the evils and oppressive bureaucratic practices which were protected by conservatives in 1937 have become a part of our administrative machinery. Yet so securely has our system of administrative tribunals become entrenched that there is no effective protest made today against bureaucratic aggression." [19]

Arnold realized that the courts had lost a great deal of ground to the bureaucracy since the 1930s. Still, he believed that the courts retained an aura of respect in American public opinion. Perhaps the recent battles over the Fortas, Haynsworth, and Carswell nominations have destroyed many of the symbols and ideals which supported that respect. Yet in the midst of the arm-twisting battle over Judge Haynsworth's nomination, the Supreme Court unanimously denied a request by the Nixon Administration to delay school desegregation in Mississippi. The rebuffed Administration publicly announced its intention to enforce the decision. Even in the wake of the Fortas, Haynsworth, and Carswell affairs, it seems premature to discount the authority and respect Arnold attributed to the courts. These judicial ordeals, however, do give fresh meaning to Arnold's observation that legal ideals "are the clothes which the Court must wear in order to retain its authority and public appearance." [20]

A second important morale-building function of legal ideals is the creation of a feeling of unity and comfort in society. Arnold asserts that "the function of law is not so much to guide society, as to comfort it." [21] Although the ideal of the "rule of law" is sometimes considered to be the moral background of revolt, it usually operates to induce acceptance of things as they are. It accomplishes this by creating a realm somewhere within the mystical haze beyond the courts, where all our dreams of justice in an unjust world come true.[22] The mystical realm of justice created by legal ideals is important to the ordinary citizen. He may be treated unjustly by a policeman at a street crossing, but chooses to pay his fine rather than go to the trouble and expense of taking his case to court. Yet he is comforted by the belief that if he did take the trouble to travel the gamut of the judicial system, he would eventually obtain justice. Even when the performance of the courts is disappointing, the citizen gains solace from the thought that there are legal principles lying beyond the courts, waiting for better judges to apply them.[23]

The heaven of legal ideals, if it is to give comfort, must remain far away. Like most utopias, its flaws become all too apparent when it gets too close to everyday life. Thus, courts, by a kind of instinctive wisdom, decide cases only after long procedural struggles during which the real cause of the litigation is forgotten. As their actions fade into a distant mist, the imperfections of the judicial process are lost.[24] The learned science of jurisprudence, which contains the principles of the law, is also sufficiently elusive to provide a heaven of comfort: "For some it lies buried in a system, the details of which they do not know. For some, familiar with the details of the system, it lies in the depth of an unread literature. For others, familiar with this literature, it lies in the hope of a future enlightenment."[25]

Arnold concluded that because Americans are in fact subject to countless petty restrictions under civil and criminal law, are subject to the nonresponsible power of private economic government, and are living in an age of rapid and inevitable centralization, they must have a judicial heaven as a dramatic and comforting representation of impersonal justice.[26]

Closely related to the feeling of social comfort is the feeling of social unity which the law fosters. According to Arnold, judicial institutions "move in all directions at once in order to satisfy the conflicting emotional values of the people. . . ."[27] The genius of the law is that it reconciles conflicting values by offering symbolic satisfaction to everyone. The least favored members of society are comforted by the fact that, under the law, the poor and the rich are treated alike. The more fortunate members of society are pleased by the fact that the wise are treated better than the foolish. The businessman is happy to find that the law protects individual freedom from governmental restraint and therefore ignores more profitable forms of dishonesty. The preacher is glad that all forms of dishonesty which can be curbed without destroying economic liberty are being curbed by the law.[28]

It is not possible for judicial institutions to admit that they are moving in many contradictory directions at the same time. Therefore, an effort must be made "to construct a logical heaven beyond the courts, wherein contradictory ideals are made to seem consistent." [29] This task is undertaken by the science of law or jurisprudence. In attempting to reconcile contradictory values, jurisprudence faced many of the same problems which confronted theology in the past. Both august disciplines were compelled to reconcile stern moral logic with benevolent and commonsense ideas. Both accomplished this feat by setting up separate categories which dramatized moral and benevolent values respectively. In theology, a separate personality known as the Redeemer appeared to represent benevolence and escape from the stern moral logic of eternal punishment for sin. The science of jurisprudence similarly conceived of separate courts of equity to escape from the stern logic of the law. Both theology and jurisprudence were able to preserve the sanctity of moral logic, and at the same time to find ways to prevent its enforcement when the result would be cruel or impractical.[30] Setting up separate categories, however, does not completely reconcile inconsistencies in either theology or law. For theology, thriving in an age of faith, the problem was not difficult to solve. Doubters were told that the ways of Providence were beyond human understanding. Jurisprudence, thriving in an age of reason, had a more difficult task: to unify inconsistent legal practices by producing an apologetic literature so complicated and unreadable that no one could discover its inner contradictions.[31]

For the great mass of people, who cannot even pretend to read jurisprudence, the reconciliation of conflicting values is accomplished through the public trial. This dramatic event permits the public to discuss all the various contradictory attitudes about crime, since they are all represented by various persons playing different roles in the trial. "Without the drama of the public trial," observes Arnold, "it is difficult to imagine on just what institution we would hang our conflicting ideals of public morality." [32]

The Constitution is also an effective instrument for creating a feeling of social unity. It is universally revered as the product of exceptionally gifted forebears who were able to write down the fundamental principles of social organization. Of course, the founding fathers could not anticipate all future contingencies, and so their written words must be supplemented from time to time by learned men who apply the fundamental principles of the Constitution to contemporary situations. This process is defended by pointing out that the forefathers wanted the Constitution to be a growing and not a static thing. On the other hand, if learned men are opposed to a new constitutional interpretation, they point out that the Constitution cannot be one thing today and another thing tomorrow. The Supreme Court uses both arguments on different occasions.[33] The Constitution thus becomes a flexible instrument that can be used on both sides of any moral question. According to Arnold, this is its great genius: "It is essential to constitutionalism as a vital creed that it be capable of being used in this way on both sides of any question, because it must be the creed of all groups in order to function as a unifying symbol." [34]

Although Arnold was convinced that the law must serve as a unifying symbol in society, he was not always consistent as to the role of the judge in creating an atmosphere of consensus. Writing in 1937 in defense of President Roosevelt's plan for reorganizing the Supreme Court, Arnold chastised the court for its internal dissension: "When a court which is supposed to represent the ideal of the rule of law and the symbol of national unity becomes a bitter battle ground between opposing political theories, the only remedy is to appoint men on the court who are sufficiently aware of the function the court must play among American ideals to exercise adequate judicial statesmanship." [35]

Twenty-three years later, Arnold was defending the Warren Court against the charge that its internal dissensions were causing it to lose the respect of "first rate lawyers." Arnold rejected the suggestion that the Justices spend more time in conference to reach a broader and clearer consensus. "Men of positive views," he said, "are only hardened in those views by such conferences." [36] A proliferation of concurring and dissenting opinions should be expected from a court made up of men who have deep-seated convictions about national problems and have taken sides on controversial issues. The conflicts on the court, concluded Arnold, "are making the Court responsive to the demands of a rapidly changing economy." [37]

It is not surprising that Arnold should change his argument over a twenty-three year period characterized by significant changes in American society and in the outlook of the Supreme Court. Arnold, with the advantage of hindsight, was glad that Roosevelt's Court Reorganization Plan failed in the unique way it did, i.e., preserving the revered symbol of an independent judiciary while at the same time helping to terminate judicial resistance to economic change. Had Roosevelt's plan succeeded, Arnold argued, "the Court would not today be our most effective symbol of freedom and human rights." [38]

Arnold's inconsistent statements about the role of judges as symbols of national unity, however, probably reflect more than the passage of time in a changing world. Arnold never reconciled completely the judge's role as the embodiment of unbiased reason and national unity with his own temperament as a partisan advocate. In fact, his reason for retiring from the Circuit Court of Appeals in 1945 was that his preference for partisan argument over impartial deliberation made him an unsuitable ornament for the judicial bench.[39] The nature of Arnold's dilemma appears most clearly in the following passage:

> The effectiveness of the law consists in the fact that there is a consensus that it represents a rational process, devoid of personal bias or prejudice. . . . This is another way of saying that if you do not believe that men are endowed with the ability to exercise unbiased free will, and are able to make decisions along the line of inexorable logic, you will not make a good judge.[40]

Because the law is able to make room for a large number of conflicting values, it performs a third important function in society: the creation of an atmosphere of tolerance. According to Arnold, judicial institutions are "the great storehouses of those contradictory notions which allow people to be different." [41] Whenever a people is swept off its feet by single-minded devotion to an ideal, judicial institutions lose prestige. They regain it only when society becomes able to tolerate contradictory ideals. "Therefore," observed Arnold, "the law is a barometer of the spiritual contentment of a people. . . ." [42] For "only when men are secure are contradictory social values tolerated." [43] The public trial is enormously important as a symbol of society's tolerance of different social values: "So important is the public trial to the whole ideological structure of any government that the adoption of more efficient and speedy ways of punishing individuals is a sure sign of instability and insecurity and decay." [44]

Arnold's appreciation of law as an expression of tolerance of contradictory ideals is related to his theory of orderly and gradual social change. Sudden revolutionary changes inspired by single-minded idealists are, for him, too costly in terms of individual liberty. Arnold expects peaceful social change to be characterized by intellectual confusion. He observes that "the more illogical the process of social change is, the less disorder and repression accompany it." [45]

If law is to embody social tolerance, it must be vigorous in its defense of civil liberties. In *The Symbols of Government*, Arnold clearly states his view of the Supreme Court's role in relation to economic theory on the one hand, and to civil liberties on the other. If the court chooses to stand guard over an economic theory, Arnold contended, it takes a dangerous gamble on the continuance of that theory. Because of the changing nature of economic theory, the court should "hesitate to interfere with any exercise of governmental power which is sincere in its purpose and honestly designed as an experiment in social welfare." [46] The ideal of a fair trial, which embodies tolerance of dissenting ideas, has far greater durability than any economic theory: "It is here that the Court can take a bold stand without gambling on the future, because the ideal of a fair trial for the oppressed has survived every dictatorship that the world has ever known." [47]

Arnold also pointed out that property interests will either have sufficient political strength to protect themselves, or be so weak that not even the court can maintain their privileges. The fanatics, the lowly, and the oppressed, however, have only the court to protect them when they wish to publicly express their ideas without undergoing punishment.[48] Thus, Arnold concluded, the court should give priority to the protection of civil liberties over the protection of economic interests: "In the celebration of legal and economic theories the Court should be equipped only with prayer books and collections of familiar quotations. In the protection of those seeking a fair trial it should be armed with a sword which it dared to use with courage." [49]

The Warren Court, Arnold observed, has given priority to the protection of civil liberties over the perpetuation of economic theory. During the Depression, judges assumed that property was more important than human rights. The Constitution of that day "stood as an unyielding obstacle to practical legislation attempting to relieve human needs and correct social injustices. . . ." [50] However, the old Constitution has gone and a different kind of Constitution has taken its place: "The new Constitution stands as a vision of racial equality, civil rights, and human freedom. It is no longer available as a weapon against social reform of any kind." [51]

After taking note of the Warren Court's decisions with respect to the administration of criminal law, the civil rights of Blacks, and the reapportionment of state legislatures, Arnold concluded: ". . . the Court has emerged triumphant, having made the greatest contribution in our judicial history since John Marshall in 1803 first established the power of the Supreme Court to declare the acts of Congress unconstitutional in *Marbury* v. *Madison*. . . ."[52]

Arnold's commitment to a tolerant, libertarian society was manifested by his views on a wide variety of civil liberties issues. He was a spirited defender of the individual's right of privacy against intrusive devices such as wiretapping. Wiretapping, to Arnold, "is the equivalent of putting a man in the bedroom to listen to everything that is said in the privacy of your house."[53] Never neglecting an opportunity to buttress his views with conservative credentials, Arnold supported his argument against wiretapping by quoting an editorial from the *Wall Street Journal*. The editorial contended that while a law to make wiretap evidence acceptable in Federal courts might not violate the *letter* of the Fourth Amendment, it could easily violate its *spirit*.[54] It is interesting that Arnold employed the very "spirit over the letter" argument that had irked him when it was used in 1937 by the opponents of President Roosevelt's Court Reorganization Plan. At that time, he observed sarcastically that the great virtue of the argument was that it could be used on both sides of any moral question without the user being bothered by what the Constitution actually says.[55] When defending the values of tolerance and individual liberty, Arnold became morally inspired in much the same way that the philosophers of 1937 became inspired defending conservative legal and economic theory.

Arnold was likely to use a variety of argumentative devices in defense of civil liberties. As a judge on the Circuit Court of Appeals, he couched an opinion defending literary freedom in the rhetoric of free trade. The Postmaster General had revoked the second-class mailing privileges of *Esquire* magazine on the ground that he considered it "morally improper and not for the public welfare." Judge Arnold noted that Congress had established the second-class mailing privilege to encourage literary contributions to the public good. But he could not agree that the Postmaster General's action had fostered this objective: ". . . the American way of obtaining that kind of contribution is by giving competitive opportunity to men of different tastes and different ideas, not by compelling conformity to the tastes or ideas of any government official." [56]

Arnold noted that Justice Holmes had expressed this idea in his famous dissent in *Abrams* v. *United States*. Holmes had said that ". . . the ultimate good desired is better reached by free trade in ideas, —that the best test of truth is the power of the thought to get itself accepted in the competition of the market." [57] Mail service, contended Arnold, provides a vital highway over which business must travel, and the rates charged for the use of this highway must not discriminate between competing businesses. If the Interstate Commerce Commission, for example, were to give lower rates only to businesses which it thought contributed to the public welfare, its action would be clearly unconstitutional. "Such a situation would involve freedom of competitive enterprise. The case before us involves freedom of speech as well." [58]

As a detached observer of society, Arnold was aware of the symbolic power that certain forms of argument have over the public. It would be erroneous to conclude, however, that he used these arguments in the fashion of a cynical manipulator. Arnold noted that even the detached, fact-minded observer is moved by inspirational forces. Thus Arnold, while aware of the symbolic and dramatic character of the ideal of a free economy or the ideal of civil liberties, was himself caught up in the inspirational drama of these ideals. The factor which kindled Arnold's enthusiasm for certain ideals was their positive relationship to his personal standard of a tolerant and humanitarian society.

The fourth function of legal ideals in society, according to Arnold, is to dramatize humanitarian values; and in his thinking, these values overlapped considerably with the libertarian value of tolerance. However, he did distinguish between the two types of values when he pointed out that a society which pursues a humanitarian ideal to the exclusion of all others will be intolerant and oppressive.

Arnold contended that the legal ceremony of a fair trial, which dramatizes both tolerance and humanitarian ideals at the same time, is of tremendous importance to society. It is true that its delays and technicalities frustrate society and that in times of great public fear, its machinery is seldom strong enough to protect weak and harmless persons. Yet the ideal of the fair trial is worth all these social costs "because of its contribution to the ultimate survival of a great humanitarian ideal." [59] When the ideal of the fair trial is violated, the dramatic effect is enormous: "Harmless anarchists may be shot by the police in a strike. Liberals will be sorry and forget. But let them be unfairly treated by a court . . . and, before the dissatisfaction has died away, the prejudice or phobia which created the unfair atmosphere of the trial will receive a public analysis and examination which otherwise it would not get." [60]

The fair trial puts before the public a moving drama wherein a great government treats the lowliest criminals as equal antagonists, strips itself of executive power, and submits the case to twelve ordinary men. The whole ceremony gives concrete representation to the humanitarian ideals of human dignity and equality. [61]

Arnold compared the fair trial to the miracle or morality plays of ancient times. The great importance of "these moving dramas on the courtroom stage" is that they "tend to create a more compassionate society." [62] The ideal of the fair trial "involves the humanitarian notion that the underdog is always entitled to a chance." [63] One of the most moving dramas on the courtroom stage in recent years, Arnold believed, was the case of *Gideon* v. *Wainwright*.[64] Gideon, a fifty-year-old man who had been convicted of four previous felonies, had been denied counsel at the trial for his last offense. The refusal was based on a holding by the Supreme Court in *Betts* v. *Brady* [65] that counsel for the accused was not necessary in state trials for minor offenses. Gideon wrote the court a letter, which he called a "petition of certiorari," from a Florida prison. Although his petition was not technically correct, the court agreed to review his case and ended by reversing its decision in *Betts* v. *Brady*.

Arnold believed that the dramatic impact of the *Gideon* decision was enormous even though thousands of persons in penitentiaries whose future might be affected by it would probably never hear of it. The idea that the distinguished judges of the highest court in America would reach down into a Florida prison to secure the rights of a lowly, habitual criminal was so moving that it became the theme of a best-selling book entitled *Gideon's Trumpet*.[66] In addition, Arnold said, a nationwide television network devoted a full hour of its prime time to a dramatic portrayal of the case. "I doubt if any of the millions of people who saw this presentation of a great moral issue were not deeply moved." [67]

Arnold believed that the dramatic presentation of the fair trial has more than a fleeting emotional impact. It tends to foster a more compassionate clinical attitude toward crime in place of a sterner moral attitude. The compassionate view crime as a disease rather than as a moral offense and concentrate on removing conditions of social deprivation rather than relying on punitive methods.[68] At this point, Arnold's conception of the fair trial was juxtaposed to his expansionary economics based on government spending for pressing social needs: ". . . the important thing needed is the recognition of a national obligation to remove the misery and economic destitution into which criminals are born. Once that obligation is accepted, the goods and services to meet it can easily be forthcoming from the constantly increasing productive capacity of the twentieth century industrial revolution." [69]

For the fair trial to dramatize humanitarian ideals, it must meet certain standards, and Arnold's writings during the 1930s contain discussions of certain celebrated trials in which he elaborated on his own conception of a fair trial. A procedure is fair, he was convinced, if the accused is given a full opportunity to present his defense and if the facts and assumptions on which the court bases its decision are fully reported in the record. By these standards, the celebrated trial of Joan of Arc by a medieval court was an outstanding example of fairness. The court gave Joan every opportunity to present her defense. So fully were the arguments in her defense considered, that her later fame rests largely on the evidence found in the trial record itself.[70] Joan was found guilty, not because of an unfair trial but because the court "was compelled to represent the prevailing ideals and phobias of its era." [71] The most important function of a fair trial, asserted Arnold, is to leave a record by which the injustice done to harmless people by the blind phobias of an age can be examined: "Where a court allows all the relevant facts to appear on the record, we may well forgive unfortunate results caused by human prejudices. Where a court denies this . . . leaving to outsiders the burden of disclosing all the facts . . . then only is the rather splendid ideal of a fair trial in danger." [72]

By this standard, according to Arnold, the trials of Benjamin Gitlow and Eugene Debs were also fair trials since the assumptions on which their convictions rested were clearly stated in the record. In the case of Gitlow, the assumption was that peace could not be secured if persons like Gitlow were allowed to talk. Debs was convicted on the theory that war could not be carried on if Debs were allowed to talk. Although these assumptions may have been unreasonable, the trials of Gitlow and Debs were fair. "No judicial machine," Arnold wrote, "is likely to question the underlying assumptions of the government which it supports, however regrettable those assumptions may be." [73]

The famous Scottsboro trial in Alabama, on the other hand, did not meet the standards of a fair trial. Arnold maintained that the Alabama court did not have sufficient confidence in the reasonableness of its assumptions to spread them frankly on the record. Had it dared to say that, as a matter of principle, Negroes were not entitled to sit on juries and that Negroes who had intercourse with white women were to be treated as white men who committed rape, then the trial would have been fair, even if the Negroes had been convicted. These assumptions remained hidden, however, and "the trial became a maze of attempts to keep relevant material out of the record." [74]

The standards of a fair trial which Arnold elaborated in 1935 were different from those he advocated during the 1950s when the McCarthy-inspired loyalty probes had reached their peak. Arnold was no longer willing to concede that a trial of a man's views and opinions could be fair. Men could only be fairly tried for their actions, not for their beliefs or their dangerous tendencies. A character or heresy trial, asserted Arnold, could not conceivably be a fair trial. Therefore, it was as impossible to devise a fair procedure for a loyalty hearing as it was for the medieval court to devise a fair trial for Joan of Arc. That court made a tremendous effort to be fair, but failed to realize "that to try a man's character or his opinions flies in the face of due process itself." [75] That Arnold had, without comment, considerably broadened his earlier conception of a fair trial is indicated by his statement in 1935: ". . . all the arguments in favor of Jeanne [Joan of Arc] were so carefully set out and answered, that as soon as prosecutions for heresy no longer fitted into popular prejudices, this trial, *so eminently fair,* appeared to be unfair.[76]

The depth of Arnold's commitment to the ideal of a fair trial was manifest in his response to the wave of loyalty probes that were ruining the careers of many innocent persons. Arnold's law firm agreed to defend such persons free of charge. Writing to Robert Hutchins in 1952, Arnold observed:

> At the present time the situation of anyone charged with Communist activities, however innocent he may be, is very precarious. Mr. Lattimore is a good example. He has not the means to defend himself or even to pay for the transcript of the proceeding. We of course

take his and all other cases for nothing and, if necessary, put up expenses, but the burden on an individual firm is very great.[77]

The ideal of a fair trial is so important to society that institutions must be required to live up to its substance as well as its form. "Any tribunal," Arnold wrote, "which takes on the trappings and aspects of a judicial hearing . . . must conform to our judicial traditions, or sooner or later it will develop into a monstrosity that demands reform." [78]

Where a legal ideal has definite humanitarian significance, Arnold insisted that it *guide* institutions as well as comfort them. The fair trial is another of Arnold's humanitarian exceptions to his early axiom that ideals exist to give morale, not direction, to institutions. Another exception, noted in Chapter IV, is his humanitarian version of the ideal of a free economy.

Most legal ideals, in Arnold's view, remain far removed from the world of practice. He cited the ideal of law enforcement as an example, carefully distinguishing it from practical measures to preserve public safety and convenience. In its abstract form, the ideal asserts that the prosecutor's duty is to enforce all the laws with equal vigor regardless of his own views of public safety and convenience. The prosecutor can do no such thing in practice because there are more laws than he could ever enforce. He views the laws as an arsenal of weapons which he can use selectively to incarcerate certain individuals who are dangerous to society. He may seek compromises with a large number of unimportant offenders to avoid clogging the courts with prosecutions. On the other hand, he may press a prosecution for some minor offense to remove a dangerous criminal from society.[79] The practical approach of the prosecutor is worlds apart from the ideal of law enforcement which distrusts bargaining with offenders, demands uniform sentences, and emphasizes laws rather than individuals.[80] The ideal compels prosecutors, officers, and judges to make the necessary compromises of criminal cases *sub rosa* while the process is openly condemned.[81]

Arnold's observations concerning law enforcement point to an important problem which he believed is endemic to legal institutions, i.e., how to reconcile the inconsistencies between legal ideals and institutional practice. Above all, the notion of a seamless web of legal principles applied by impartial judges according to the dictates of reason must be reconciled with contradictory practices. The conventional method for supporting the "seamless web" idea, observed Arnold, is by an elaborate ceremony of learning and research. "Books piled on books give us a vision of the impartiality of legal learning, and the possibility of its constant improvement toward the end of abstract justice." [82] The science of jurisprudence supplies the deficiencies of law as a rational process by applying more reason. The result is an enormous amount of argumentative literature.[83] The law schools also make an important contribution to the ceremony of learning and research: "Harvard is busy collecting books, giving scholarships to persons who are willing to read them, and employing professors to read what the scholarship students have written." [84]

Arnold was convinced that there is a more satisfactory way of reconciling legal ideals with the actual workings of legal institutions which would curb the inflation of legal literature. The best approach to this problem is to emphasize a science *about* law, which would include in its subject matter the narrower science *of* law.[85] Arnold's science *about* law would consider the law in the same way that a detached anthropologist would observe the customs of a primitive culture. The traditional science *of* law includes all the morale-building ceremonies and ideals of the law. Arnold clarified his hopes for a science *about* law by comparing it to the Copernican revolution. Once men ceased to think of the earth as the center of the universe and began looking at it from the outside, amazing advances in man's control over the physical environment were made possible. Similarly, if law is viewed from the perspective of the world surrounding it rather than as the center of an independent universe, it can be used as a means of social control.[86]

The main problem facing Arnold's science *about* law is one of peaceful coexistence with the science *of* law. Arnold himself saw that those who take legal ceremonies and ideals to be literal truths will be disturbed by observations made from an anthropological perspective. It would seem that a professor lecturing at Yale about the seamless web of the law could not help being disturbed by the knowledge that, across the hall, Arnold was comparing his beliefs to the rituals of a primitive culture. Arnold, however, insisted that peaceful coexistence is possible. The science *about* law, he said, does not "involve abandoning the proverbs, parables, and precepts of the law." It means only that lawyers should think differently about the law when they are on "the solemn judicial stage" than when they are off it. "Once diagnosis becomes

a recognized technique," concluded Arnold, "the orator and the drama-
tist will find that their place in the law is still undisturbed." [87]

Arnold's critics, however, remain skeptical that legal philosophy can
coexist with an anthropological approach which denies its objective validity. Georges Gurvitch, for example, contends that, by reducing legal
ideals to subjective projections and illusions, Arnold undermined the
"objective and spiritual values" which inspire those ideals. Gurvitch contends that the "philosophy of law" can coexist with the "sociology of
law" only if both recognize that there is at least some objective validity
in the values and ideals which inspire the law. The major difference between Gurvitch's two concepts of law and those of Arnold is that Gurvitch is able to partially unite the philosophical and sociological dimensions of law through their common acceptance of a realm of objective
moral values upon which both must draw. Arnold's sciences *of* law and
*about* law, on the other hand, operate on entirely different assumptions, and must pursue independent objectives unless one is to be absorbed by the other. Gurvitch implies that this is the result of Arnold's
approach which, he contends, "returns to the earlier imperialism of
sociology." [88]

Many of Arnold's own observations would induce skepticism about
his hope for peaceful coexistence between the science *about* law and the
science *of* law. For example, Arnold was of the opinion that all vital
creeds must be believed as literal truths. If they are viewed as folklore
rather than as truth, legal creeds can be expected to lose their vitality.
Arnold himself seemed to recognize this fact in a letter written to an
acquaintance in 1960: "Senator Taft . . . used to tell me that he
thought it was a good thing to have one fellow like myself on the Yale
Law Faculty but he certainly wouldn't want many more of them. There
is some truth in what he said." [89]

"My own way of expressing the paradox," Arnold wrote, "is to say
that if people generally agreed with what I said, nothing I said would be
any longer true." [90] It would seem that unconventional observations
like those of Arnold cannot succeed in dividing the study of law into
two distinct approaches based on contradictory assumptions. Rather,
the genius of jurisprudence finds ways of incorporating the contributions of men like Arnold without altering its overall moral conception
of the law. Thus, thinkers of Arnold's caliber, too gifted to be ignored,

had to be content to see legal philosophy move ever so slowly toward their perspectives, incorporating bits and pieces of their philosophy in such a way as not to cause serious indigestion to the body of jurisprudence. Arnold's vision seems to have been a science *about* law, incorporating and—at the same time—preserving the science *of* law. But jurisprudence, in its infinite genius for reconciliation and survival, usually succeeds in incorporating the science *about* law rather than being incorporated by it.

Arnold, along with other dissenters in the legal profession, has left his skeptical mark on American jurisprudence. The nature of his individual contribution can be further explored by comparing him with three of the most important dissenting legal thinkers of the twentieth century—Oliver Wendell Holmes, Jr., Roscoe Pound, and Jerome Frank.

Holmes viewed the law primarily in terms of physical force. He focused upon "the circumstances in which public force will be brought to bear upon men through the courts." [91] Arnold, on the other hand, emphasized the *psychological* rather than the *physical* force of the law. The results of this difference in emphasis by Holmes and Arnold can be seen in their respective approaches to the adjustment of group differences and the protection of individual rights in society.

"I believe," wrote Holmes, "that force, mitigated so far as may be by good manners is the *ultima ratio,* and between two groups that want to make inconsistent kinds of world I see no remedy except force. . . ." [92] Arnold's approach to the reconciliation of conflicting social ideals was quite different. Force, he thought, is "too exhausting" to maintain social unity over a long period of time. This task can only be performed by symbols and ideals that are generally accepted and extremely flexible.

As a judge, Holmes most assuredly attempted to civilize force by the "good manners" of democratic rules, but his conception of the *ultima ratio* of social adjustment led him to view the law primarily as a method of umpiring social battles. Arnold, on the other hand, emphasized the unifying function of the law, which is able to reduce social conflict by offering symbolic satisfaction to many groups in many different ways.

Holmes considered force to be the ultimate basis of individual rights as well as the ultimate basis of adjustment between conflicting groups. "Just so far as the aid of the public force is given a man, he has a legal right. . . ." [93] Arnold's observations again reveal a dimension which Holmes has overlooked. The right of a fair trial, for example, was significant to Arnold not because of the *application* of public force, but because of the voluntary *suspension* of public force by the state while twelve ordinary men determine the outcome according to their respective lights. In relatively stable times, the ideal of a fair trial is supported, not so much by public force as by widespread emotional attachment to the values dramatized through this moving judicial ceremony.

Arnold's emphasis on the psychological impact of law in society was also quite different from Holmes's narrowly focused interest in the concrete results of legal contests. "The prophesies of what the courts will do in fact," Holmes said, "and nothing more pretentious, are what I mean by the law." [94] To understand the law, Holmes recommended viewing it from the perspective of the "bad man" whose interest lies in guessing how his particular case will be decided.

Arnold's discussion of the importance of the *Gideon* case illustrates his departure from Holmesian guidelines. He dismissed the importance of the decision for the thousands of convicts directly affected (Holmes's "bad men") and emphasized its impressive psychological impact on society.

These distinctive approaches might be summarized as a difference between Holmes's *positivism* (connoting an emphasis on physical force and concrete judicial behavior—the more readily observable and measurable aspects of the legal process) and Arnold's *psychologism* (connoting an emphasis on law was a psychological force in society—a less readily observable and measurable aspect of the legal process).

A second important distinction can be drawn between the Darwinian tendencies of Holmes and the humanistic tendencies of Arnold. "I shall think socialism begins to be entitled to serious treatment," wrote Holmes, "when, and not before, it takes life in hand and prevents the continuance of the unfit." [95] The doctrines of Malthus appealed to Holmes. He once remarked that he would "let Malthus loose" on those who contributed neither "thought nor beauty to life." [96] As a justice on the Supreme Court, he gave legal expression to these views in an opinion upholding compulsory sterilization of inmates in institutions for the feebleminded.[97]

Arnold's clear preference for those legal ideals which protect powerless and oppressed groups in society is a contrast to Holmes's tough-minded approach to the law. The contrast, however, should not be over-drawn. Holmes was, on balance, a strong defender of the civil liberties of minorities; nevertheless, he leaves the impression that his defense of civil liberties does not derive so much from a belief in the dignity of the individual as from a desire to keep minorities intact so that they will not lose their fair chance to become the dominant force in society. "The sacredness of the individual," Holmes remarked, "is a purely municipal ideal of no validity outside the jurisdiction." [98] Arnold, on the other hand, praised the "fair trial" as a concrete expression of the ideals of individual dignity and equality. These ideals, as embodied in the fair trial, have "survived every dictatorship that the world has ever known." Holmes prided himself on detachment from humanitarian considerations.[99] Arnold's legal philosophy was permeated with them.

One of the great achievements of Holmes's "detached" and "hard-boiled" jurisprudence was the identification of law with the will of the majority. This represented an enormous gain over the traditional notions of abstract and timeless legal principles which in practice served to fortify special interests seeking to preserve the economic status quo. The task of further broadening the social base of the law was undertaken by Roscoe Pound. Pound's philosophy reaches out boldly beyond Holmes's majority interest to identify law with the satisfaction of as many social interests as possible. "The pressure of the unsecured interest or unsatisfied demand," said Pound, "keeps us at work trying to find the more inclusive solution." [100] The creative work of lawmakers and judges in finding more inclusive social solutions is Pound's idea of "social engineering." The task involves the adjustment of overlapping and conflicting interests as well as an attempt to broaden overall social satisfactions.

Arnold's writings incorporate the central tenets of Poundian philosophy and thus reinforce the identification of law with more inclusive social objectives. Like Pound, Arnold's theory was pluralistic rather than majoritarian. Society was conceived as a complex of different interests to be satisfied. Both Pound and Arnold sought to offer "something for everybody" through the law, and both set out to accomplish this by creative social engineering.

Pound's theory of social interests, however, is open to the criticism that it does not attach sufficient importance to the civil liberties of individuals. To be sure, the important civil liberties are listed among Pound's sixty categories and subcategories of social interests,[101] but there is nothing to suggest the importance that should be assigned them in relation to the numerous other interests listed. The protection of civil liberties, therefore, is made to depend on a precarious balancing process with no guidelines to indicate the extent of that protection. The practical result of such a "balancing test" is likely to be the weakening rather than the strengthening of judicial protection of civil liberties.[102]

Like Pound, Arnold viewed the law as a means of satisfying and reconciling many conflicting interests. But he departed from Pound by strongly advising judges to give priority to the protection of civil liberties. Although Arnold never admitted it, he introduced a moral conception of justice and individual rights into a legal theory purporting to deal only with morale. In his later writings, this moral commitment is more evident. For example, he asserted in 1955 that "the philosophy of justice" must stand over the conflicting ideals of society, keeping each in its proper place. The ideal of the fair trial, symbolizing the priority of the rights of the individual to those of the state, must prevail over "every consideration of efficiency in government administration." [103]

Although Roscoe Pound devoted his considerable energies to bringing law into a closer relationship with the social sciences, he stopped far short of allowing the social sciences to govern his conception of the nature and function of law.[104] However, Arnold and another bold iconoclast, Jerome Frank, were not hesitant in taking this step. Both men brought psychology to the forefront of legal analysis. They concluded that the realm of legal ideals serves the psychological function of comforting society rather than the practical function of guiding it.

Frank contends that legal thinking is guided by the "basic myth" of certain and unchanging law. The need for legal certainty can be traced to the child's need for an absolute authority figure. The role of the father—giving the appearance of certainty in an uncertain world—is transferred in adulthood to the law. Arnold, in similar fashion, sees law offering emotional comfort by creating the illusion of justice in an unjust world.

Although Frank and Arnold agreed on the mythical nature and psychological function of legal ideals, they disagreed on what should be done about it. Frank insists that law must be liberated from its childhood fixation as soon as possible. Arnold, on the other hand, believes that legal myths serve positive social functions and should not be discouraged.[105] Frank strongly disagrees with Arnold's view that legal illusions should be retained for some imagined social purpose after they have been unveiled by perceptive critics.[106] Society is only harmed by continued adherence to childish illusions. The legal critic must have the courage to help society "grow up." Lack of courage, Frank concedes, is not usually the reason why perceptive critics do not wish to overturn legal illusions. He offers a more subtle explanation which contains some important insights into the legal philosophy of Arnold. "Such men . . . are still in some small part enthralled by the myths they have learned to see through . . . they . . . cannot bear to have the shams utterly exposed, the superstitions totally destroyed. They find a lingering comfort in the spectacle of a public still under the spell." [107]

The impression left by Arnold's legal writings bears a strong resemblance to Frank's diagnosis. Arnold was willing to let extralegal perspectives govern his diagnosis of the law, yet he found "the idea of federal judges roaming the stormy fields of economics, sociology, psychiatry, and anthropology, their black robes flapping in the winds of controversy . . . a disquieting one. . . ." [108] Arnold did not believe that law is a "brooding omnipresence in the sky" and yet he thought it important that the general public so conceive it. He satirized the notion that judicial decisions are the product of detached reason, but contended that a good judge should believe in it. He exposed the unrealistic quality of legal ideals but asserted that if men do not strive for them the law loses its "moral force."

Arnold explained his reluctance to abandon legal ideals by pointing to the importance of their stabilizing and unifying impact on society. The reader, however, cannot escape the impression that these ideals provided a certain amount of comfort and inspiration for Arnold himself; and that he would have been most disturbed if his skeptical views had been completely accepted by the legal profession.

Arnold's insights into the psychological significance of the law point to important deficiencies in Frank's "adult jurisprudence." Arnold realizes that the legal ideals Frank would attack constitute the psychological basis for the prestige of judicial institutions. He doubts that the concept of the "adult personality" is sufficiently inspiring to replace the legal ideal of authoritative impartial law.[109] Arnold's point is well taken. If the general public ceased to believe that the judgments of courts were more impartial and certain than those of legislative bodies, it is doubtful that the present importance and independence of courts in the American system of government could be maintained.

Both Frank and Arnold are open to criticism for emphasizing only the psychological and mythical aspects of legal ideals. Certainly the guiding ideal of "a government of laws and not of men" is contradicted countless times in practice. But if the phrase were completely discredited and the discretionary standard "a government of men and not of laws" put in its place, it seems probable that the exercise of arbitrary authority would increase. If a legal standard is capable of inspiring a people, it is likely to find expression in reality as well as in poetry. When ideals find only partial expression in society, it is no more "realistic" to regard them as myths than it is to regard them as literal truths.

Arnold's exclusive concern with the symbolic and psychological properties of law renders his theory of little use as a tool for understanding and dealing with the kind of radical disrespect for law which is manifested today by the destructive rioting of slum Blacks. This explosive problem makes it clear that the law must offer concrete as well as symbolic satisfaction to all groups in society if it is to retain respect. In his recent writings, Arnold—without much elaboration—related his legal philosophy to the concrete needs of disadvantaged groups.[110] His *personal* commitment to meeting these needs was always evident. This does not alter the fact that his theory of law, developed during the 1930s, is exclusively concerned with the psychological and symbolic benefits of the law.

Charles A. Reich addresses himself to more concrete legal issues in a recent article dealing with the legal rights of welfare recipients—many of whom live in the slums.[111] The Social Security Act conferred certain rights which (as Arnold would be quick to observe) symbolized a new public attitude toward welfare recipients. Reich contends, however, that in practice these rights are virtually unprotected and frequently violated. Entitlements granted by government to other social groups, e.g., professional licenses, farm subsidies, contracts for defense, space, and education are not neglected in this fashion. "It is only the poor whose entitlements, although recognized by public policy, have not been effectively enforced." There is a great danger to society, concludes Reich, "when any group in the population lacks entitlements and hence chronically suffers from insecurity and dependence." [112] He urges the legal profession to become actively involved in social welfare to provide concrete enforcement of rights granted three decades ago but still largely ignored.

Arnold's theory of legal ceremonies and symbols does not begin to come to grips with the kind of problem Reich describes, nor does it tend to inspire the kind of concrete legal action he recommends. Despite this serious limitation, Arnold's psychologically oriented theory of law was a genuine contribution to American legal theory. The reverence for law in American society is a matter of faith based only partially on concrete experience. Arnold's imaginative account of how this faith is preserved by symbols and ceremonies and how it, in turn, preserves social unity was an important as well as an original contribution to our understanding and appreciation of American law. When men come to regard law purely as a public convenience, Arnold will cease to be relevant; but as long as they continue to project their ideals onto the legal system, Arnold's insights will be helpful.

# NOTES

[1] Thurman Arnold, "The Role of Substantive Law and Procedure in the Legal Process," *Harvard Law Review*, vol. 45 (February 1932), p. 630.   [2] Ibid.
[3] Ibid., *Folklore of Capitalism*, p. 79.   [4] Ibid., p. 67.
[5] Ibid., "Book Review—Soviet Administration of Criminal Law by Judith Zelitch," *Columbia Law Review*, vol. 32 (May 1932), p. 924.   [6] Ibid.
[7] *Home Building and Loan Association* v. *Blaisdell.* 290 U.S. 398 (1934); *Nebbia* v. *New York.* 291 U.S. 502 (1934); *Ryan* v. *Panama Refining Co.* 293 U.S. 388 (1935).
[8] Arnold, *Symbols of Government*, p. 175.   [9] Ibid., p. 193.
[10] *Schechter Poultry Corp.* v. *United States.* 295 U.S. 495 (1935).
[11] Arnold, *Symbols of Government*, p. 177.   [12] Ibid., p. 182   [13] p. 189   [14] p. 190   [15] p. 194   [16] pp. 201–02.
[17] Ibid., "Trial by Combat and the New Deal," *Harvard Law Review*, vol. 47 (April 1934), p. 944.
[18] Ibid., "The Folklore of Capitalism Revisited," p. 193.   [19] Ibid., pp. 193–94.
[20] Ibid., "Professor Hart's Theology," *Harvard Law Review*, vol. 73 (May 1960), p. 1311.
[21] Ibid., *Symbols of Government*, p. 34.   [22] Ibid., pp. 34–35   [23] p. 223.
[24] Ibid.   [25] pp. 58–59   [26] pp. 224–25   [27] p. 49   [28] p. 35.
[29] Ibid., p. 56   [30] pp. 61–62   [31] pp. 65–66   [32] pp. 147–48.
[33] Ibid., *Folklore of Capitalism*, p. 28.   [34] Ibid., p. 29.
[35] Ibid., "A Reply (in Support of the President's Supreme Court Plan)," *American Bar Association Journal*, vol. 23 (May 1937), p. 368.
[36] Ibid., "Professor Hart's Theology," p. 1312.   [37] Ibid., pp. 1313–14.
[38] Ibid., *Fair Fights and Foul*, p. 69.   [39] Ibid., p. 159   [40] p. 61.
[41] Ibid., *Symbols of Government*, p. 242.   [42] Ibid., pp. 247–48   [43] p. 130.
[44] Ibid., "The American Ideal of a Fair Trial," *Arkansas Law Review*, vol. 9 (summer 1955), pp. 311–12.
[45] Ibid., *Symbols of Government*, p. 247.   [46] Ibid., p. 196   [47] p. 197.

48 Ibid.   49 pp. 197–99.

50 Ibid., *Fair Fights and Foul*, p. 68.   51 Ibid.   52 p. 75.

53 Ibid., "Wiretapping: The Pros and Cons," *New York Times Magazine* (November 29, 1953), p. 28.   54 Ibid., p. 12.

55 Ibid., *Folklore of Capitalism*, p. 29. See also Arnold, "A Reply (in Support of the President's Supreme Court Plan)," p. 367.

56 *Esquire* v. *Walker*. 80 U.S. App. D.C. 145. Decided June 4, 1945, pp. 146–47.

57 *Abrams* v. *United States*. (1919) 250 U.S. 616 at 630. Quoted by Arnold in *Esquire* v. *Walker*, p. 147.

58 *Esquire* v. *Walker*, pp. 147–48.

59 Arnold, *Symbols of Government*, pp. 142–43.   60 Ibid., p. 142.

61 Ibid., p. 145. See also Thurman Arnold, "Book Review—*The Story of My Life* by Clarence Darrow," *Yale Law Journal*, vol. 41 (April 1932), p. 932.

62 Ibid., *Fair Fights and Foul*, pp. 231, 245.   63 Ibid., p. 228.

64 *Gideon* v. *Wainwright*. 372 U.S. 335 (1963).

65 *Betts* v. *Brady*. 316 U.S. 455 (1942).

66 Anthony Lewis, *Gideon's Trumpet* (New York: Random House, 1964).

67 Arnold, *Fair Fights and Foul*, p. 243.   68 Ibid., pp. 235, 244–45   69 p. 245.

70 Ibid., *Symbols of Government*, p. 135.

71 Ibid., p. 141   72 pp. 140–41   73 p. 140   74 pp. 141–42.

75 Ibid., "The American Ideal of a Fair Trial," p. 314.

76 Ibid., *Symbols of Government*, p. 141. Emphasis mine.

77 Ibid., *Selections from Letters and Legal Papers of Thurman Arnold*, p. 75.

78 Ibid., "Mob Justice and Television," *Atlantic Monthly*, vol. 187 (June 1951), p. 70.

79 Ibid., *Symbols of Government*, p. 153. See also Arnold, "Law Enforcement—An Attempt at Social Dissection," pp. 17–18.   80 Ibid., p. 154   81 p. 162.

82 Ibid., *Fair Fights and Foul*, p. 259.

83 Ibid., "Apologia for Jurisprudence," *Yale Law Journal*, vol. 44 (March 1935), p. 731.

84 Ibid., *Fair Fights and Foul*, p. 270.

85 Ibid., "Institute Priests and Yale Observers—A Reply to Dean Goodrich," *University of Pennsylvania Law Review*, vol. 84 (May 1936), p. 822.

86 Ibid., pp. 823–24.

87 Ibid., "The Jurisprudence of Edward S. Robinson," p. 1288.

88 Georges Gurvitch, *Sociology of Law* (London: K. Paul, Trench, Trubner and Co., Ltd., 1947), p. 144; see also pp. 1–2, 146–47, 240–41.

89 Arnold, *Selections from Letters and Legal Papers of Thurman Arnold*, pp. 52–53.

90 Ibid., p. 53.

91 Quoted by John C. Ford, "The Fundamentals of Holmes' Juristic Philosophy," in Francis Le Buffe and James Hayes, *The American Philosophy of Law* (New York: Crusader Press, 1947), p. 378.

92 Mark De Wolfe Howe (ed.). *The Holmes-Pollock Letters*, vol. II (Cambridge: Harvard University Press, 1941), p. 36.

93 Holmes, *The Common Law*, p. 214.   94 Quoted in Max Lerner, *The Mind and Faith of Justice Holmes* (New York: Modern Library, 1943), p. 75.

95 Ford, "Fundamentals of Holmes' Juristic Philosophy," p. 397.   96 Ibid., p. 396.

[97] *Buck* v. *Bell.* 274 U.S. 200 (1927).

[98] Howe, *Holmes-Pollock Letters,* p. 36.

[99] Lerner, *Mind and Faith of Justice Holmes,* pp. 45–46.

[100] Roscoe Pound, *Interpretations of Legal History* (New York: Macmillan, 1923), p. 157.

[101] See Reuschlein, *Jurisprudence—Its American Prophets,* pp. 142–44.

[102] See Justice Frankfurter's majority opinion in *Minersville School District* v. *Gobitis* 310 U.S. 586 (1940) and his concurring opinion in *Dennis* v. *United States* 341 U.S. 494, at 525.

[103] Arnold, "The American Ideal of a Fair Trial," p. 311.

[104] For example, Pound abandoned the idea of deriving the categories of social interest from the motivational concepts of social psychology and based them instead on claims made upon the legal system.

[105] This difference of opinion led to characteristic differences between the two men in their exercise of the judicial function. Compare Judge Frank's opinion in *United States* v. *Roth* 237 F. 2d 796, 801–27 with Judge Arnold's opinions in *Holloway* v. *United States* 148 F. 2d 665 and *Fisher* v. *United States* 149 F. 2d 28.

[106] See Judge Frank's remarks on Demogue and Wurzel in *Law and the Modern Mind* (New York: Tudor Publishing Co., 1935), pp. 223–31.   [107] Ibid., p. 235.

[108] Thurman Arnold, "Judge Jerome Frank," *University of Chicago Law Review,* vol. 24 (summer 1957), p. 634.   [109] Ibid.

[110] Ibid., *Fair Fights and Foul,* pp. 244–45.

[111] Charles A. Reich, "Individual Rights and Social Welfare: The Emerging Legal Issues," *Yale Law Journal,* vol. 74 (June 1965), pp. 1245–57.   [112] Ibid., p. 1255.

# CHAPTER VI

# CONCLUSIONS

The undermining of established systems of thought by the dissenting intellectuals of the late nineteenth and early twentieth centuries [1] was strongly reinforced by the writings of Thurman Arnold, especially those which appeared in the 1930s. By undermining the conservative orthodoxy of their time, the dissenters, including Arnold, also undermined the philosophical tenets of eighteenth-century Jeffersonian liberalism which supported individualism, minimal government, and the beneficence of natural economic laws. Yet Jefferson and the dissenters had certain common purposes which point to what is perhaps the most enduring characteristic of American liberalism.

Arthur Schlesinger has observed that the basic meaning of American liberalism from Jefferson to the New Deal lies in the effort by less powerful elements in American society to control the business community, ordinarily the most powerful.[2] More specifically, liberalism has usually enlisted farmers, small entrepreneurs, and laborers to check the concentration of politico-economic power in the hands of organized business interests.

Jeffersonian liberalism was animated by its opposition to Hamilton's policy of national subsidization of manufacturing, mercantile, and investing interests at the expense of agrarian interests. Jefferson thought of big government chiefly as an agency for giving unfair advantages to wealthy businessmen. Thus, the predominant strain of Jefferson's economic thinking was *laissez faire*. He was inclined to believe that the natural economic order was beneficent and should not normally be disturbed by government.

By the 1830s the gap between Jeffersonian theory and economic reality had widened considerably. Corporations in banking, transportation, and manufacturing were becoming more powerful and influential. President Andrew Jackson came to realize that only by increased government intervention in the affairs of business could the growing concentration of wealth and power be effectively checked. As Schlesinger observes, "For the Jeffersonians, mistrust of banks and corporations was chiefly a matter of theory; for the Jacksonians, it was a matter of experience." [3] Although Jackson recognized the need for greater governmental intervention in business affairs, he justified these actions as attempts to restore the natural economic order. He adhered in theory to the *laissez faire* principles of Adam Smith, as had Thomas Jefferson who considered *The Wealth of Nations* "the best book extant" on economic questions.[4]

Industrial capitalism underwent unprecedented expansion in the decades following the Civil War. The imposing size and power of new business organizations, however, made little impact on prevailing economic theory. The classical economics of Adam Smith became deeply embedded in the schools and colleges of the post-Civil War period. The philosophical lag which was noticeable during Jackson's presidency became chronic during the closing decades of the nineteenth century. At a time when rapid and massive economic change was the dominant characteristic of the American scene, economic theory continued to emphasize static laws. Academic economists conceived of the universe as a closed system operating in accordance with unchanging universal laws. The static laws of economics were thought to be beneficent provided they were not interfered with by government. The influence of static *laissez faire* thinking was strengthened rather than weakened by the evolutionism of William Graham Sumner who contended that the social order was fixed by natural laws "precisely analogous to those of the physical order."

Any extension of government activity into economic affairs could only mar the flawless operation of these laws.

During the closing decades of the nineteenth century, constitutional law increasingly reflected the influence of *laissez faire* economic theory. Thomas M. Cooley, the leading authority on American constitutional law during this period, gave great impetus to this development. By identifying the constitutional clause, "due process of law," with the protection of property rights, he performed a great service to lawyers and judges seeking to embody *laissez faire* in American constitutional law.[5] As the Constitution became more and more a bulwark of property, conservative judges and lawyers interpreted it as the embodiment of fixed and changeless principles. They saw their task as one of discovering these principles and defending them against the pernicious tendencies of social and economic legislation.

By the 1890s, conservative theorists had succeeded in identifying the industrial capitalism distrusted by Jefferson with the natural economic order he championed. Eighteenth-century liberal ideas were transformed into conservative systems of thought which protected business organizations from liberal reformers seeking to check their politico-economic power.

Liberal intellectuals of the 1890s began to range themselves against the philosophical trends which they believed could serve only conservative purposes. They revolted against what Morton White has called "formalism" in American thought, i.e., its abstract, rationalistic, static orientation.[6] From the 1890s to the 1930s (when Thurman Arnold's most important writings appeared) criticisms of both the methods and conclusions of conservative social thought grew in extent and influence.

The dissenting intellectuals of the late nineteenth and early twentieth centuries found that many of the tenets of Jeffersonian philosophy had to be altered if not discarded. Individualism, they insisted, must be understood in terms of social groups and organizations. The concept of a natural economic order must be partially or completely discarded to make room for deliberate regulation and/or planning by government.

Although the dissenters altered or discarded many tenets of Jefferson's philosophy, they shared his desire to check the politico-economic power of organized business interests and his distrust of abstract philosophies which had lost contact with personal and social experience. The attitude of religious homage toward the Constitution or toward economic theories was as foreign to Jefferson's thought as it was to the thought of the dissenting intellectuals.

To dissolve the "steel chain" of conservative ideas, the dissenters attacked the notion of absolute, universal, and unchanging ideas in all fields of social thought. Thurman Arnold reinforced the attack on absolutes by asserting that ideas are relative to organizations. It is not the duty of organizations to follow principles but rather the purpose of principles to serve organizations. The priority of organizations, however, is not unqualified. Arnold provided an explicit standard by which organizations and creeds can be judged: ". . . in order to make judgments as to whether any activity is a good or a bad thing, it is necessary to have standards. For the time being we are adopting the standard that it is a good thing to produce and distribute as much goods as the inventive and organizing genius of man makes possible." [7]

Interpreters and critics of Arnold's major writings too often overlook this explicit standard. Max Lerner, for example, observes that Arnold provided a theory of tactics without revealing the ends those tactics are to serve.[8] Sidney Hook contends that Arnold's loyalty to organizations rather than principles left no basis for judging organizations other than the effectiveness of the techniques of political control.[9] Both of these criticisms overlook Arnold's explicit statement of a standard by which both organizations and techniques can be judged.

Lerner and Hook, however, make the valid observation that Arnold inadvertently admitted moral values, which are not explicitly stated, into his writings. For example, Arnold asserted that institutions should be judged "by their utility in the distribution of physical comforts *and in the development of an attitude of spiritual peace.*" [10] We have previously seen (Chapter II) that "spiritual peace" was related in Arnold's thinking to tolerance, a second standard to which he was strongly committed. Arnold's discussion of the importance of a fair trial makes it clear that he placed a moral value on tolerance and fairness to individuals as individuals *quite independently* of the contribution of this ideal to the production and distribution of material wealth. Arnold also went beyond his purely materialistic standard when he warned that fanatical devotion to a single ideal stifles "kindness" and "makes human liberty an unimportant value." Moral principles, which Arnold declared inimical to objective analysis in certain passages, became subtly but surely integral parts of his analysis in other passages.

Arnold's major writings have an unfortunate tendency to undermine the objective validity of principles which might play a serious and constructive role in society as well as those which are retrogressive. Nowhere did Arnold draw a distinction between realistic and unrealistic ideals. He assumed that all ideals will be unrealistic, and he concerned himself solely with the problem of employing them constructively.

His approach dismissed the possibility of mitigating the effects of philosophical lag by developing a more realistic set of ideals. Practical men are left with only one alternative: the manipulation of myths. Arnold's emphasis on manipulation might have been an appropriate tactic during periods of ideological transition such as the 1930s, but it fails to recognize the necessary task of replacing outworn ideals with new principles designed to be taken seriously as guides to a meaningful social existence.

Arnold and the dissenting intellectuals who preceded him employed a variety of methods intended to encourage critical analysis in social studies. They examined social institutions from the detached perspective of the anthropologist, the evolutionary perspective of the historian, and the holistic perspective of the generalist. Arnold employed all these perspectives in a series of cogent observations which ignored the standard approaches and conventional boundaries of established academic disciplines.

In place of a systematic theory consisting of formal definitions and logical progressions, Arnold offered numerous illustrative examples which invite the reader to view prevailing ideals and institutions in unaccustomed ways. Thus, he did not attempt to define the essence of private corporations, but simply observed that they are "like armies." This observation could be subjected to innumerable intellectual criticisms. It lacks precision, exaggerates, overgeneralizes, has no specific content, and is in great need of elaboration. These criticisms, however, do not speak to Arnold's main purpose which was not to detail the distinguishing characteristics of private corporations, an exercise his readers would rapidly forget, but to bring his audience to view private corporations in a new way, i.e., as disciplined, authoritarian organizations rather than as competing individuals.

Arnold's illustrations were characterized by cogency, imagination, and humor. They reach across historical epochs and disciplinary boundaries simultaneously to provide illuminating parallels to prevailing social institutions. Thus, Arnold described medical controversies in the Middle Ages to satirize conservative resistance to the economic measures of the New Deal. He poked fun at modern legal textbooks by comparing them to earlier theological treatises such as *Bush on the Resurrection, Plenary Inspiration, Cases on Conscience,* and *Method of Divine Government.*[11]

Arnold's talent was displayed in his imaginative use of history rather than in his mastery of it. C. Wright Mills has said of Marx and Weber that "every line they write is soaked in knowledge of history. They have truly assimilated it." Other thinkers such as Mosca and Durkheim "tend more to use it, at times rather externally, as illustrations of this or that theory." [12] Arnold's approach to history fell in Mills's second category. It is the approach of a brilliant amateur: amateurish, because Arnold was more a dabbler in history than a master of it; brilliant, because of the skill and imagination with which Arnold used history to communicate new meanings.

In common with the dissenting intellectuals of the late nineteenth and early twentieth centuries, Arnold preferred to concentrate on the whole of society rather than its fragmented parts. He deplored the artificial division of social phenomena into separate categories called "law," "economics," "sociology," and "political science." Rather than polite chatting across disciplinary boundaries, Arnold advocated making the boundaries themselves less distinct.

Arnold's holistic approach amounted in practice to a consortium of intellectuals who were generalists like himself; men whose interests in broad social trends and problems took them far afield from the discipline in which they received their professional training. For example, Arnold deeply respected men such as Edward S. Robinson, a psychologist who became a member of the Yale Law School faculty and developed a psychological theory of jurisprudence; Walton Hale Hamilton, a distinguished institutional economist who also joined the Yale law faculty; Charles Horton Cooley, a pioneer in sociology who had received his doctorate in economics; and Leon Keyserling, a graduate of Harvard Law School, who became an economic adviser to President Truman.

Generalists such as Arnold had difficulty giving their strongest loyalties to the insular concerns of their respective disciplines. They are frequently looked upon with some disfavor by the stauncher members of their disciplines as "armchair philosophers," "popularizers," or "gadflies." This disfavor is not completely undeserved. The generalist always runs the risk of brilliant superficiality. As Charles Horton Cooley, commenting on changes in sociology, observed: "We elders 'got by' and now would like to raise standards. When everybody was trying to do everything we were all so superficial that no one ventured to cast stones at any one else. But the new generation will not tolerate 'armchair' sociology." [13]

Brilliant superficiality, however, seems a price worth paying for the fresh insights frequently provided by broad-ranging generalists. During the 1930s, the very elaborate disciplines of law and economics were remarkably insulated from the world of social change around them. Arnold's brilliant but superficial plunges into history and psychology provided a critical assessment of the intellectual products of academic orthodoxy. He noted the similarities between the dialectics of legal theorists and the reasonings of theologians. He compared respectable economists to Roman augurs who studied the entrails of geese, and always seemed to find bad omens for legislation which they disliked. He observed that legal and economic theories were similar to the deceptive rationalizations of mental patients. These broad-ranging observations dramatized the failure of prevailing legal and economic theories to realistically assess the social trends and problems of the 1930s.

The critical perspectives of Arnold and the dissenting intellectuals of the late nineteenth and early twentieth centuries were intended in large part to clear the way for social reform. The dissenters were in agreement with John Dewey's contention that the sanctification of *a priori* universal principles was a major obstacle to the kind of thinking necessary to secure intelligent social reforms. Even Oliver Wendell Holmes, who was as skeptical of reformers as he was of businessmen, believed that legal principles should not be absolutized in such a way as to block social experimentation.

Thurman Arnold's two major books, *The Symbols of Government* and *The Folklore of Capitalism,* were masterpieces in satirical analysis of the great conservative systems of thought which made reform so difficult in the 1930s. The "atmosphere of religious worship" surrounding these systems and the business institutions to which they gave "mystical" support was the primary target of Arnold's corrosive satire. Although the "practical observations" contained in Arnold's books do much to clear the way for reform thinking, they offer little in the way of specific programs to implement reform. Arnold remained remarkably aloof from the disagreements which existed within the New Deal over programs and policies. He did not discuss the practical issues raised by these disagreements; i.e., the merits and proper scope of national planning, the groups which should or would control the process of planning, the merits and proper scope of various schemes of direct regulation, government subsidies, government corporations, or the restoration of competition (aside from some satirical remarks on the operational failures of the antitrust laws). He merely observed that expanded governmental organizations were needed to "fill in the social gaps" left by the "industrial feudalism."

Arnold's neglect of specific programs of reform reflects the fact that his major concern was the *psychological* rather than the technical or managerial problems of reform. In common with the dissenting intellectuals before him, he emphasized the application of scientific intelligence to human problems. Most of the dissenters, however, were interested in the *programmatic* use of the scientific method; i.e., the use of scientific techniques to diagnose social needs, devise programs based on this objective diagnosis, and finally to test the effectiveness of the programs in action. Arnold's overriding interest, on the other hand, lay in the *psychological* use of the scientific method; i.e., the use of scientific techniques to discover the impact of emotionally charged words and beliefs on human behavior, and to apply these findings by manipulating slogans devised to *gain public acceptance* for new programs.

Most of the dissenting intellectuals recognized the irrationality of prevalent ideals and institutional practices, but their response was to encourage widespread acceptance of an objective scientific attitude toward social institutions and problems. Arnold dismissed this effort as futile. He contended that irrational myths would continue to be the moving forces of political life and should be manipulated for humanitarian purposes.

Arnold stated that his psychological approach to reform draws support from the discoveries of modern psychiatry which can be profitably applied to human institutions. These discoveries, according to Arnold, reveal that various ideals within the human personality are contradictory to each other and to the behavior of the individual. Psychiatrists have learned to accept the irrational ideals of their patients and to manipulate them to achieve the patient's physical comfort. In similar fashion, concluded Arnold, the politician should accept the irrational nature of social ideals and manipulate them to make the members of society more comfortable.

Arnold's advice to the politician, however, was based on a misunderstanding of the purposes of modern psychiatry. The psychoanalyst, for example, sees his task as "Helping the client to become more aware of his unconscious feelings . . . [resulting in] more spontaneity, rationality, and other values implicit in the mature personality." [14] The analyst does not try to manipulate irrationality, but rather to *reduce* it by bringing it before conscious inspection.

Unlike Arnold, modern psychiatrists do not accept an inevitable contradiction between ideals and behavior. "When behavior and the basic philosophy of life are at odds," observe the authors of a widely respected text on psychotherapy, "the personality usually is in trouble." [15] Rather than uncritically accepting and manipulating irrational ideals, the modern psychiatrist helps his patient toward the development of a "tested personal philosophy adequate for his time and circumstances." [16] The perspectives of modern psychiatry, therefore, do not support Arnold's approach to reform so much as they support the approach taken by most of the earlier dissenting intellectuals who, recognizing the irrationality of social ideals and behavior, sought to reduce it by encouraging an attitude of scientific objectivity toward the social problems and institutions of their times.

Arnold's emphasis on social control by manipulation of irrational symbols and ideals separates him from most of his fellow American dissenters and gives him much in common with a group of European thinkers—sometimes referred to as "the Machiavellians"—all of whom stress the irrationality of politics and the inevitability of elite rule.[17] Arnold can be differentiated from this group primarily in terms of his characteristically American faith in reform through democratic (albeit manipulated) politics. He ascribes far less importance to the role of violence as a means of social control than do European thinkers in the "Machiavellian" tradition.

If Arnold's elitism is somewhat tame by European standards, it is quite bold by American standards. To be sure, contemporary American political scientists are far more "elite conscious" than were most of their predecessors of the 1930s.[18] Arnold anticipated this contemporary trend in political science and, mostly to his disadvantage, moved boldly beyond it.

The most prominent characteristic of contemporary "elitist theories of democracy," contends Professor J. L. Walker in a recent essay, is the tendency to view elites as the bulwark of liberal democratic values, in contrast to classical theories of democracy which placed primary importance upon the attitudes of the general public.[19] The late V. O. Key provides a good example of this viewpoint. "The critical element for the health of a democratic order," he maintained, "consists in the beliefs, standards, and competence of those who constitute the influentials, the opinion leaders, the political activists in the order." [20] Arnold, in a similar vein, advised his readers not to fear chaos and oppression from new organizations as long as the men who direct them "are good organizers and at the same time tolerant and humanitarian." The values of a society are determined, according to Arnold, by the creed of the class in power or by the creed of a new class rising to power. Thus, for Arnold as for Key, the character of elites was the critical element for the health of a democracy.

The point at which Arnold went beyond the elitism of contemporary political scientists is found in the extent to which he believed public opinion could be controlled by scientific manipulation. Professor Walker points out that in most of today's "elitist theories of democracy . . . it is assumed that the individual citizen will receive information from several conflicting sources, making it extremely difficult for any one group to 'engineer consent' by manipulating public opinion." [21] Arnold, on the other hand, contended that political "games can be controlled" once the relationships between social symbols and human behavior are discovered by social scientists and applied by politicians. Arnold's hope represented a naive belief in the near omnipotence that can be derived from the findings of modern social science. A small but representative sample of these findings is contained in a recent survey of public opinion by Lane and Sears.[22] On the basis of conclusions drawn from scientific studies in this area, the authors offer certain canons of advice to politicians—two of which are presented below:

1. On any given issue, the greater the change in opinion you advocate, the greater will be the audience change—*if* the audience respects you highly *and* if it has relatively weak convictions on the matter.
2. On any given issue, the greater the change in opinion you advocate, the more you will be criticized and the less change you will get—*if* the audience already has strong opinions on the issue, and is somewhat indifferent to you as an advocate.[23]

These axioms suggest that there are sharp limits to the powers of social control which politicians can expect to garner from a careful study of the recent findings in the social sciences. Arnold not only underestimated the enormous difficulty of building a body of knowledge sufficiently subtle, complex, and flexible to constitute a science of social control; he also overlooked the unpleasant fact—emphasized by contemporary political scientists—that effective social control would require stifling the flow of information from opposing sources. In other words, Arnold overlooked the basic incompatibility between his elitist theory of social control and his libertarian sentiments.[24]

Perhaps the closest parallel in recent American political science to Arnold's bold elitist and manipulatory concepts is found in the early writings of Harold D. Lasswell. Arnold and Lasswell both began with the assumption that individuals are poor judges of their own best interests and have an "infinite capacity" for making ends of their symbols. Lasswell made his assumption explicit,[25] whereas Arnold clearly implied it in his notion of the basic inconsistency between the ideals of individuals and their "practical needs."

On the basis of this assumption, both Lasswell and Arnold were quite skeptical of the value of extensive public discussion and debate in society. "Discussion," asserted Lasswell, "frequently complicates social difficulties, for the discussion by far-flung interests arouses a psychology of conflict which produces obstructive, fictitious, and irrelevant values." [26] Arnold agreed that public debate hardened existing opinions around fictitious and irrelevant ideals, making practical compromise much more difficult. Both Arnold and Lasswell minimized the contribution of public debate to objective diagnosis and treatment of real social problems.

Rather than extending public discussion or facilitating the expression of group interests, Lasswell and Arnold proposed to channel the power of violent divisive emotions into relatively harmless symbolic channels by skillful manipulation of slogans and myths. The task of manipulation was to be performed by a new elite characterized by a new attitude toward social institutions.[27]

There is great danger to democratic institutions in both the assumptions and the conclusions shared by Arnold and Lasswell. The notion that individuals are poor judges of their own interests is usually accompanied by the belief that some uniquely qualified group can more effectively determine their interests for them. Arnold's "fact-minded observers" and Lasswell's "social scientists" are assumed to have such capabilities. Once the view is accepted that an elite is more capable of determining the best interests of the average citizen than is the average citizen himself, the political procedures for registering popular demands and reactions become primarily an *obstacle* to good government rather than a necessary ingredient of it. The logical conclusion is that democratic procedures (if they are to be maintained at all) function best when they are under the manipulatory control of a qualified elite.

The unique qualification of Lasswell's and Arnold's elites lies in their scientific detachment. Both men believed that modern social scientists can study human organizations and prescribe cures as disinterestedly as a physician diagnoses and treats a patient. This assumption is certainly open to serious question. Is Lasswell, a social scientist, completely disinterested when he links the hope of the world with the skills of his profession? [28] Was Arnold merely an "objective observer" when he described the rise of a new leadership class (consisting of fellow New Dealers)? It seems most improbable that any group of men, including social scientists, can exercise political power with the dispassionate attitude of the physical scientist. There is no evidence that the research methods developed by social scientists have rendered them immune from the pleasures of prestige and dominance which have led other elites to abuse their power.

In the light of these considerations, it is to Arnold's credit that the objectives of his theory of social control were considerably less ambitious than are those of Lasswell. Arnold's interest in psychological manipulation was confined to gaining public acceptance for social and economic reforms designed to maintain the material prosperity of the nation. Beyond this limited objective, Arnold had no desire to adjust the psychological attitudes of individuals. Lasswell, on the other hand, views politics as a kind of mass psychotherapy.[29] Unlike Arnold, he links politics directly to the mental health of individuals. Politics is to be concerned with promoting healthy psychic states among political participants and ordinary citizens alike. Political science will be allied with fields concerned with the individual's mental health, e.g., general medicine, psychopathology, and physiological psychology.[30]

Arnold's theory of social control was less ambitious than Lasswell's in geographical scope as well as in psychological application. Arnold was seeking solutions only for American problems, and had no vision of permanent cures. Lasswell, on the other hand, is searching for a permanent reduction of world tension through the agency of a universal body of myths and symbols.[31]

Although Arnold's prescriptions were bolder than those of most reform-minded American dissenters, his purposes (especially when compared to those of Lasswell) did not seem radically different. Like American reformers before him, Arnold was concerned with limiting the power of organized business interests and clearing the way for more governmental intervention in the economy. He represented the extreme liberal reaction to conservative preemption of doctrines used earlier by Jefferson and Jackson to check the social power of dominant business groups. If businessmen have successfully used Jeffersonian doctrines in an irrational way, Arnold reasoned, then liberals must do the same. Public manipulation rather than public education is the surest means of securing reform in a nation dominated by irrational myths.

Yet whether he intended it or not, Arnold's writings during the 1930s served the purpose of public education. They popularized the facts of the corporate revolution uncovered by other writers, and exposed the discrepancy between these facts and the prevailing ideals of law and economics. Although Arnold professed indifference to the development of a more "realistic" set of ideals, his critical dissection of social "folklore" was a valuable point of departure for those who wished to pursue this purpose. By exposing the fanciful dimensions of ideals accepted as absolute and unchanging truth, he facilitated more realistic trends in social thought.

In addition to undermining conservative folklore, Arnold provided observations of lasting significance concerning the interplay of ideals and institutions. His cogent demonstration of the importance of a friendly ideological climate to the growth and development of institutions is as applicable today as it was during the 1930s. It helps explain, for example, how organizations associated with the Department of Defense have been able to undertake programs involving huge sums of money with relatively little controversy, while new organizations associated with President Johnson's War on Poverty must operate in an atmosphere of intense controversy to secure relatively meager sums. Arnold also provided a valuable conceptual framework for looking into the future. Speculations about tomorrow's social ideals, he asserted, should be based on close observation of today's rising organizations. This advice is helpful in appreciating the significance of the growth of the "warfare industry" since World War II,[32] the anticipated expansion of the "knowledge industry," [33] and the growing demand for expansion of public service organizations to grapple with long neglected social problems. Arnold's insights in contemporary context add a new dimension to the importance of public policy decisions relating to the competing claims of these institutions.

Arnold continued over the years to espouse his views in books, articles, and speeches. His contribution to American social thought, however, is found mainly in his writings during the 1930s, which contain the richest supply of original and probing ideas. His later writings add important insights into his deepest moral and political commitments, and clarify some of the puzzling ambiguities of his earlier works. The important message contained in Arnold's writings throughout the years is that the emotional force of ideals must be channeled into practical humanitarian purposes if those ideals are to withstand the test of time. Hopefully, this message will not be ignored by the proponents of business ideals or by the scientifically inspired intellectuals who are increasingly assuming the responsibilities of social leadership.

## NOTES

[1] The methods and conclusions of these thinkers are reviewed in Chapter I.

[2] Arthur M. Schlesinger, Jr., *The Age of Jackson* (Boston: Little, Brown & Co., 1945), p. 505.  [3] Ibid., p. 313  [4] pp. 314–15.

[5] Benjamin R. Twiss, *Lawyers and the Constitution* (Princeton, N.J.: Princeton University Press, 1942), pp. 25–26.

[6] Morton White, *Social Thought in America—the Revolt Against Formalism* (Boston: Beacon Press, 1957), pp. 11–12.

[7] Arnold, *Folklore of Capitalism*, p. 177.

[8] Lerner, "The Shadow World of Thurman Arnold," p. 702.

[9] Hook, "The Folklore of Capitalism: The Politician's Handbook—a Review," p. 344.

[10] Arnold, *Folklore of Capitalism*, pp. 137–38. Emphasis mine.

[11] Ibid., *Symbols of Government*, p. 67.

[12] C. Wright Mills, ed., *Images of Man* (New York: George Braziller, Inc., 1960), p. 13.

[13] Edward C. Jandy, *Charles Horton Cooley: His Life and Social Theory* (New York: Dryden Press, 1942), p. 241.

14 Lawrence M. Brammer and Everett L. Shostrom, *Therapeutic Psychology* (Englewood Cliffs, N.J.: Prentice-Hall, Inc., 1960), p. 31.

15 Ibid., p. 389   16 p. 390.

17 See James Burnham's study of the common elements in the philosophies of Machiavelli, Pareto, Sorel, Mosca, and Michels: *The Machiavellians* (Chicago: John Day Company, 1943).

18 The striking exception to this generalization is found in the early writings of Harold D. Lasswell: see *Politics—Who Gets What, When, How* (New York: McGraw-Hill, 1936); and *Psychopathology and Politics* (Chicago: University of Chicago Press, 1930).

19 Jack L. Walker, "A Critique of the Elitist Theory of Democracy," *American Political Science Review*, vol. 60 (June 1966), pp. 285–95.

20 V. O. Key, *Public Opinion and American Democracy* (New York: Alfred A. Knopf, 1961), p. 558.

21 Walker, "A Critique of the Elitist Theory of Democracy," p. 286.

22 Robert E. Lane and David O. Sears, *Public Opinion* (Englewood Cliffs, N.J.: Prentice-Hall, Inc., 1964).   23 Ibid., p. 49.

24 In recent years Arnold recognized this incompatibility and expressed his distrust of government by manipulation of symbols. (See Chapter II.)

25 Lasswell, *Psychopathology and Politics*, pp. 194–95.   26 Ibid., pp. 196–97.

27 See Lasswell's proposal for a "politics of prevention," ibid., pp. 196–203.

28 See Lasswell, *World Politics and Personal Insecurity* (Chicago: University of Chicago Press, 1934), p. 20.   29 Ibid., p. 233.

30 Lasswell, *Psychopathology and Politics*, p. 203.

31 Ibid., *World Politics and Insecurity*, p. 237.

32 See Galbraith, *The New Industrial State*.

33 Kenneth E. Boulding, "The Knowledge Boom," *Challenge*, vol. 14 (July/ August 1966), pp. 5–7.

# BIBLIOGRAPHY

## PRIMARY SOURCES—Thurman Arnold

### Books

Arnold, Thurman W. *The Bottlenecks of Business.* New York: Reynal & Hitchcock, 1940.

————. *Cartels or Free Enterprise?* Public Affairs Pamphlet No. 103. New York: Public Affairs Committee, 1945.

————. *Democracy and Free Enterprise.* Norman: University of Oklahoma Press, 1942.

————. *Fair Fights and Foul.* New York: Harcourt, Brace & World, Inc., 1965.

————. *The Folklore of Capitalism.* New Haven: Yale University Press, 1937.

————. *Selections from the Letters and Legal Papers of Thurman Arnold.* Collected by Victor H. Kramer. Washington, D.C.: Merkle Press, Inc., 1961.

148

Arnold, Thurman W. *The Symbols of Government.* New Haven: Yale University Press, 1935.

————— et al. *The Future of Democratic Capitalism.* Philadelphia: University of Pennsylvania Press, 1950.


*Addresses and Articles*

Arnold, Thurman W. (Address.) *Proceedings of the Nebraska State Bar Association,* vol. 38, pp. 187–94.

—————. (Address.) *Report of the Fifty-Eighth Annual Session of the Georgia Bar Association* (May 1944), pp. 135–52.

—————. "Advice to a Young Man," *Changing Times* (June 1962), pp. 17–20.

—————. "The American Ideal of a Fair Trial," *Arkansas Law Review,* vol. 9 (summer 1955), pp. 311–17.

—————. "Antitrust Activities of the Department of Justice," *Oregon Law Review,* vol. 19 (December 1939), pp. 22–31.

—————. "Antitrust Law Enforcement, Past and Future," *Law and Contemporary Problems,* vol. 7 (winter 1940), pp. 5–23.

—————. "Apologia for Jurisprudence," *Yale Law Journal,* vol. 44 (March 1935), pp. 729–53.

—————. "Bar and Law School Unite for Research in West Virginia," *American Bar Association Journal,* vol. 15 (February 1929), pp. 67–68.

—————. "Bullying the Civil Service," *Atlantic Monthly,* vol. 188 (September 1951), pp. 45–46.

—————. "The Changing Law of Competition in Public Service," *West Virginia Law Quarterly,* vol. 34 (February 1928), pp. 183–88.

—————. "The Code 'Cause of Action' Clarified by the United States Supreme Court," *American Bar Association Journal,* vol. 19 (April 1933), pp. 215–18.

—————. "The Collection of Judicial Statistics in West Virginia," *West Virginia Law Quarterly,* vol. 36 (February 1930), pp. 184–90.

—————. "Contempt-Evasion of Criminal Process as Contempt of Court," *West Virginia Law Quarterly,* vol. 34 (February 1928), pp. 188–92.

—————. "Criminal Attempts—The Rise and Fall of an Abstraction," *Yale Law Journal,* vol. 40 (November 1930), pp. 53–80.

—————. "Depression: Not in Your Lifetime," *Collier's,* vol. 131 (April 25, 1953), p. 24.

—————. "The Economic Purpose of Antitrust Laws," *Mississippi Law Journal,* vol. 26 (May 1955), pp. 207–14.

—————. "Effectiveness of the Federal Antitrust Laws," *American Economic Review,* vol. 39 (June 1949), p. 690.

—————. "Emergency Powers and the Antitrust Laws," *Missouri Bar Journal,* vol. 12, pp. 174–78.

Arnold, Thurman W. "The Folklore of Capitalism Revisited," *Yale Review,* vol. 52 (December 1962), pp. 188–204.

———. "The Folklore of Mr. Hook—A Reply," *University of Chicago Law Review,* vol. 5 (April 1938), pp. 349–53.

———. "Free Trade Within the Borders of the United States," *South Carolina Bar Association: Transactions of the 47th Annual Meeting* (April 1940), pp. 94–102.

———. "How Not to Get Investigated," *Harper's,* vol. 197 (November 1948), pp. 61–63.

———. "In Contempt of Justice," *New Republic,* vol. 150 (March 7, 1964), pp. 32–33.

———. "An Inequitable Preference in Favor of Surety Companies," *West Virginia Law Quarterly,* vol. 36 (April 1930), pp. 278–88.

———. "Institute Priests and Yale Observers—A Reply to Dean Goodrich," *University of Pennsylvania Law Review,* vol. 84 (May 1936), pp. 811–24.

———. "Judge Jerome Frank," *University of Chicago Law Review,* vol. 24 (summer 1957), pp. 633–42.

———. "Judicial Councils," *West Virginia Law Quarterly,* vol. 35 (April 1929), pp. 193–238.

———. "The Jurisprudence of Edward S. Robinson," *Yale Law Journal,* vol. 46 (June 1937), pp. 1282–89.

———. "Labor's Hidden Holdup Men," *Reader's Digest,* vol. 38 (June 1941), pp. 136–40.

———. "The Lake Cargo Rate Case of February 1928," *West Virginia Law Quarterly,* vol. 34 (April 1928), pp. 272–82.

———. "The Lake Cargo Rate Controversy," *West Virginia Law Quarterly,* vol. 34 (June 1928), pp. 365–66.

———. "Law Enforcement—An Attempt at Social Dissection," *Yale Law Journal,* vol. 42 (November 1932), pp. 1–24.

———. "The Law to Make Free Enterprise Free," *American Heritage,* vol. 11 (October 1960), pp. 52–55, 92–94.

———. "Leon Green: An Appreciation," *Illinois Law Review,* vol. 43 (March–April 1948), pp. 1–4.

———. "Mob Justice and Television," *Atlantic Monthly,* vol. 187 (June 1951), pp. 68–70.

———. "Mr. Justice Murphy," *Harvard Law Review,* vol. 63 (December 1949), pp. 289–93.

———. "Professor Hart's Theology," *Harvard Law Review,* vol. 73 (May 1960), pp. 1298–1317.

———. "Progress Report on Study of the Federal Courts–No. 7," *American Bar Association Journal,* vol. 17 (December 1931), pp. 799–802.

———. "A Reply (in Support of the President's Supreme Court Plan)," *American Bar Association Journal,* vol. 23 (May 1937), pp. 364–68.

Arnold, Thurman W. "A Reply to 'Farewell to Grand Juries in Antitrust Litigation,'" *American Bar Association Journal,* vol. 50 (October 1964), pp. 925–27.

———. "The Restatement of the Law of Trusts," *Columbia Law Review,* vol. 31 (May 1931), pp. 800–23.

———. "Review of the Work of the College of Law," *West Virginia Law Quarterly,* vol. 36 (June 1930), pp. 319–29.

———. "The Role of the Bar in War," *Illinois Bar Journal,* vol. 30 (June 1942), pp. 409–14.

———. "The Role of Substantive Law and Procedure in the Legal Process," *Harvard Law Review,* vol. 45 (February 1932), pp. 617–47.

———. "The Sherman Act on Trial," *Atlantic Monthly,* vol. 192 (July 1953), pp. 38–42.

———. "A Talk with Thurman Arnold," *Dun's Review,* vol. 88 (November 1966), pp. 10–11, 87–88.

———. "Theories about Economic Theory," *Annals of the American Academy of Political and Social Science,* vol. 172 (March 1934), pp. 26–36.

———. "This War Will Save Private Enterprise," *Saturday Evening Post* (May 30, 1942), pp. 24–25.

———. "Trial by Combat and the New Deal," *Harvard Law Review,* vol. 47 (April 1934), pp. 913–47.

———. "Walton Hale Hamilton," *Yale Law Journal,* vol. 68 (January 1959), pp. 399–400.

———. "Wesley A. Sturges," *Yale Law Journal,* vol. 72 (March 1963), pp. 640–42.

———. "What is Monopoly?" *Vital Speeches,* vol. 4 (July 1938), pp. 567–70.

———. "Wiretapping: The Pros and Cons," *New York Times Magazine* (November 29, 1953), p. 12.

——— et al. "A Discussion of 'The Ideologies of Taxation,'" *Tax Law Review,* vol. 18 (November 1962), pp. 1–22.

——— et al. "A Report to the Committee on Judicial Administration and Legal Reform of the West Virginia Bar Association Containing Suggestions Concerning Pleading and Practice in West Virginia," *West Virginia Law Quarterly,* vol. 36 (December 1929), pp. 1–102.

Arnold, Thurman W. and Walton H. Hamilton. "Thoughts on Labor Day," *New Republic,* vol. 115 (September 2, 1946), pp. 252–55.


*Book Reviews*

Arnold, Thurman W. *The Business of the Supreme Court* by Felix Frankfurter and James Landis. Reviewed in the *West Virginia Law Quarterly,* vol. 34 (June 1928), pp. 408–10.

# Thurman Arnold, Social Critic

Arnold, Thurman W. *Conflicting Penal Theories in Statutory Criminal Law* by Mabel A. Elliott. Reviewed in the *Illinois Law Review,* vol. 26 (February 1932), pp. 719–22.

———. *The Elements of Crime* by Boris Brasol. Reviewed in the *West Virginia Law Quarterly,* vol. 34 (June 1928), pp. 410–13.

———. *Essays in Jurisprudence and the Common Law* by Arthur L. Goodhart. Reviewed in the *Yale Law Journal,* vol. 41 (December 1931), pp. 318–20.

———. *Ford on Evidence.* Reviewed in the *Yale Law Journal,* vol. 45 (March 1936), p. 959.

———. *How to Conduct a Criminal Case* by William H. Black. Reviewed in the *Yale Law Journal,* vol. 39 (May 1930), pp. 1083–84.

———. *Judge and Jury* by Leon Green. Reviewed in the *Yale Law Journal,* vol. 40 (March 1931), pp. 833–35.

———. *Jural Relations* by Albert Kocourek. Reviewed in the *West Virginia Law Quarterly,* vol. 35 (December 1928), pp. 98–99.

———. *Law of Engineers and Architects* by Lawrence P. Simpson and Essel R. Dillavow. Reviewed in the *West Virginia Law Quarterly,* vol. 35 (April 1939), pp. 298–99.

———. *The Law of Martial Rule* by Charles Fairman. Reviewed in the *Harvard Law Review,* vol. 45 (December 1931), pp. 400–02.

———. *Law of Trusts and Trustees* by George G. Bogert. Reviewed in the *Columbia Law Review,* vol. 36 (April 1936), pp. 687–90.

———. *Precedent in English and Continental Law* by A. L. Goodhart. Reviewed in the *Columbia Law Review,* vol. 35 (February 1935), pp. 311–13.

———. *Soviet Administration of Criminal Law* by Judah Zelitch. Reviewed in the *Columbia Law Review,* vol. 32 (May 1932), pp. 923–25.

———. *The Story of My Life* by Clarence Darrow. Reviewed in the *Yale Law Journal,* vol. 41 (April 1932), pp. 932–33.

———. *Studies in Law and Politics* by Harold J. Laski. Reviewed in the *Columbia Law Review,* vol. 33 (February 1933), pp. 377–78.

———. *A Treatise on the Law of Oil and Gas* by Walter L. Summers. Reviewed in the *West Virginia Law Quarterly,* vol. 34 (June 1928), pp. 413–15.

———. *The Trial of Jeanne D'Arc* by W. P. Barrett. Reviewed in the *Yale Law Journal,* vol. 42 (January 1933), pp. 459–62.

*Judicial Opinions of Thurman Arnold—Associate Justice of the Court of Appeals for the District of Columbia: March 16, 1943–July 10, 1945*

Bailey v. Zlotnick. 149 F. 2d, 505; 80 U.S. App. D.C. 117 (1945).
Better Business Bureau v. United States. 148 F. 2d, 14; 79 U.S. App. D.C. 380 (1945).

*Blake* v. *Trainer.* 148 F. 2d, 10; 79 U.S. App. D.C. 360 (1945).

*Cook* v. *Cook.* 135 F. 2d, 945; 77 U.S. App. D.C. 388 (1943).

*Cromer* v. *United States.* 142 F. 2d, 697; 78 U.S. App. D.C. 400 (1944).

*Davy* v. *Crawford.* 147 F. 2d, 574; 79 U.S. App. D.C. 375 (1945).

*De Marcos* v. *Overholser.* 137 F. 2d, 698; 78 U.S. App. D.C. 131 (1943).

*Diggs* v. *Welch.* 148 F. 2d, 667; 80 U.S. App. D.C. 5 (1945).

*Esquire* v. *Walker.* 151 F. 2d, 49; 80 U.S. App. D.C. 145 (1945).

*F. J. Stokes Machine Co.* v. *Coe.* 146 F. 2d, 866; 79 U.S. App. D.C. 325 (1945).

*Fisher* v. *United States.* 149 F. 2d, 28; 80 U.S. App. D.C. 96 (1945).

*Fox* v. *Ickes.* 137 F. 2d, 30; 78 U.S. App. D.C. 84 (1943).

*Gaston* v. *United States.* 143 F. 2d, 10; 79 U.S. App. D.C. 37 (1944).

*Griffith-Consumers Company* v. *Noonan.* 136 F. 2d, 271; 78 U.S. App. D.C. 32 (1943).

*Grome* v. *Steward.* 142 F. 2d, 756; 79 U.S. App. D.C. 50 (1944).

*Hamilton* v. *United States.* 140 F. 2d, 679; 78 U.S. App. D.C. 316 (1944).

*Hecht Co.* v. *Whiteford.* 137 F. 2d, 929; 78 U.S. App. D.C. 134 (1943).

*Hill* v. *Hawes.* 144 F. 2d, 511; 79 U.S. App. D.C. 168 (1944).

*Holloway* v. *United States.* 148 F. 2d, 665; 80 U.S. App. D.C. 3 (1945).

*Holmes* v. *F. W. Berens Inc.* 149 F. 2d, 388; 80 U.S. App. D.C. 114 (1945).

*Hoover Co.* v. *Coe.* 144 F. 2d, 514; 79 U.S. App. D.C. 172 (1944).

*Hurwitz* v. *Hurwitz.* 136 F. 2d, 796; 78 U.S. App. D.C. 66 (1943).

*James Heddon's Sons* v. *Coe.* 146 F. 2d, 865; 79 U.S. App. D.C. 317 (1945).

*Klepinger* v. *Rhodes.* 140 F. 2d, 697; 78 U.S. App. D.C. 340 (1944).

*Kraft Cheese Co.* v. *Coe.* 146 F. 2d, 313; 79 U.S. App. D.C. 297 (1944).

*Lambros* v. *Young.* 145 F. 2d, 341; 79 U.S. App. D.C. 247 (1944).

*Maloney* v. *Foundry Methodist Episcopal Church et al.* 139 F. 2d, 388; 78 U.S. App. D.C. 263 (1943).

*McKay* v. *Parkwood Owners, Inc.* 139 F. 2d, 385; 78 U.S. App. D.C. 260 (1943).

*Melvin* v. *Melvin.* 140 F. 2d, 17; 78 U.S. App. D.C. 285 (1944).

*Minnesota Mining and Manufacturing Co.* v. *Coe.* 143 F. 2d, 12; 79 U.S. App. D.C. 59 (May 1, 1944).

*Monsanto Chemical Co.* v. *Coe.* 145 F. 2d, 18; 79 U.S. App. D.C. 155 (1944).

*N.L.R.B.* v. *Central Dispensary and Emergency Hospital.* 145 F. 2d, 852; 79 U.S. App. D.C. 274 (1944).

*Neel* v. *Barbra.* 136 F. 2d, 269; 78 U.S. App. D.C. 13 (1943).

*Neely* v. *United States.* 144 F. 2d, 519; 79 U.S. App. D.C. 177 (1944).

*New York Life Insurance Co.* v. *Taylor.* 147 F. 2d, 297; 79 U.S. App. D.C. 66 (1944).

*O'Hara* v. *District of Columbia.* 147 F. 2d, 146; 79 U.S. App. D.C. 302 (1944).

*Overholser* v. *De Marcos.* 149 F. 2d, 23; 80 U.S. App. D.C. 91 (1945).

*Peter J. Schweitzer Inc.* v. *N.L.R.B.* 144 F. 2d, 520; 79 U.S. App. D.C. 178 (1944).

*Potts* v. *Coe.* 140 F. 2d, 470; 78 U.S. App. D.C. 297 (Jan. 18, 1944). 145 F. 2d, 27; 79 U.S. App. D.C. 223 (Aug. 7, 1944).

*Puget Sound Power and Light Co.* v. *Federal Power Commission.* 137 F. 2d, 701; 78 U.S. App. D.C. 143 (1943).

*Railroad Retirement Board* v. *Duquesne Warehouse Co.* 149 F. 2d, 507; 80 U.S. App. D.C. 119 (1945).

*Rainbow Dyeing and Cleaning Co.* v. *Bowles.* 150 F. 2d, 273; 80 U.S. App. D.C. 137 (1945).

*Reeves* v. *Bowles.* 151 F. 2d, 16; 80 U.S. App. D.C. 207 (1945).

*Rone* v. *Rone.* 141 F. 2d, 23; 78 U.S. App. D.C. 369 (1944).

*Russell* v. *Russell.* 142 F. 2d, 753; 79 U.S. App. D.C. 44 (1944).

*Sanders* v. *Bennett.* 148 F. 2d, 19; 80 U.S. App. D.C. 32 (1945).

*Schneider* v. *Schneider.* 141 F. 2d, 542; 78 U.S. App. D.C. 383 (1944).

*Shokuwan Shimabukuro* v. *Higeyoshi Nagayama.* 140 F. 2d, 13; 78 U.S. App. D.C. 271 (1944).

*Special Equipment Co.* v. *Coe.* 144 F. 2d, 497; 79 U.S. App. D.C. 133 (1944).

*Smith* v. *Schlein.* 144 F. 2d, 257; 79 U.S. App. D.C. 166 (1944).

*Strong* v. *Huff.* 148 F. 2d, 692; 80 U.S. App. D.C. 89 (1945).

*Tippit* v. *Wood.* 140 F. 2d, 689; 78 U.S. App. D.C. 332 (1944).

*Travelers Insurance Co.* v. *Cardille.* 140 F. 2d, 10; 78 U.S. App. D.C. 255 (1943).

*United States* v. *Carmody.* 148 F. 2d, 684; 80 U.S. App. D.C. 58 (1945).

*United States Rubber Co.* v. *Coe.* 146 F. 2d, 315; 79 U.S. App. D.C. 305 (1945).

*Urciolo* v. *O'Connor.* 149 F. 2d, 386; 80 U.S. App. D.C. 112 (1945).

*Urquhart* v. *American–La France Foamite Corp.* 144 F. 2d, 542; 79 U.S. App. D.C. 219 (1944).

*Vanderhuff* v. *Vanderhuff.* 144 F. 2d, 509; 79 U.S. App. D.C. 153 (1944).

*Walker* v. *Popenoe.* 149 F. 2d, 511; 80 U.S. App. D.C. 129 (1945).

*Waterman S. S. Corporation* v. *Land.* 151 F. 2d, 292; 80 U.S. App. D.C. 167 (1945).

*Watson* v. *Massachusetts Mutual Life Insurance Co.* 140 F. 2d, 673; 78 U.S. App. D.C. 248 (1943).

*Williams* v. *Huff.* 146 F. 2d, 867; 79 U.S. App. D.C. 326 (1945).

*Williams* v. *United States.* 138 F. 2d, 81; 78 U.S. App. D.C. 147 (1943).

*Wolpe* v. *Poretasky.* 144 F. 2d, 505; 79 U.S. App. D.C. 141 (1944).

## SECONDARY SOURCES—Other Writers

*Books*

Beard, Charles A. *An Economic Interpretation of the Constitution of the United States*. New York: Macmillan, 1935. First published in 1913.

Bentley, Arthur F. *The Process of Government*. Bloomington, Ind.: Principia Press, Inc., 1935. First published in 1908.

Berle, Adolf A. and Gardiner Means. *The Modern Corporation and Private Property*. New York: Macmillan, 1933.

Brammer, Lawrence M. and Everett L. Shostrom. *Therapeutic Psychology*. Englewood Cliffs, N.J.: Prentice-Hall, Inc., 1960.

Brandeis, Louis. *The Curse of Bigness*. New York: Viking Press, 1934.

Burnham, James. *The Machiavellians*. Chicago: John Day Company, 1943.

Cahill, Fred V. *Judicial Legislation*. New York: Ronald Press, 1952.

Clark, John Bates. *The Distribution of Wealth*. New York: Kelley and Millman, 1956. First published in 1899.

Clark, John Maurice. *Preface to Social Economics*. New York: Farrar and Rinehart, 1936.

Commons, John R. *Institutional Economics*. New York: Macmillan, 1934.

———. *Legal Foundations of Capitalism*. New York: Macmillan, 1924.

———. *My Self*. New York: Macmillan, 1934.

Curti, Merle. *The Social Ideas of American Educators*. Paterson, N.J.: Pageant Books, 1959.

Dewey, John. *Liberalism and Social Action*. New York: G. P. Putnam's Sons, 1935.

———. *The Quest for Certainty*. New York: Minton, Balch & Company, 1929.

———. *Reconstruction in Philosophy*. Boston: Beacon Press, 1957. Original edition by Henry Holt & Company, 1920.

Dorfman, Joseph. *The Economic Mind in American Civilization*. New York: Viking Press, 1949 (vol. 3), 1959 (vol. 4).

———. *Thorstein Veblen and His America*. New York: Viking Press, 1934.

Ely, Richard T. *Ground Under Our Feet*. New York: Macmillan, 1938.

Frank, Jerome. *Law and the Modern Mind*. New York: Tudor Publishing Co., 1935.

Galbraith, John Kenneth. *The Affluent Society*. Boston: Houghton Mifflin Co., 1958.

———. *The New Industrial State*. Boston: Houghton Mifflin Co., 1967.

Goldman, Eric F. *Rendezvous with Destiny*. New York: Vintage Books, 1956.

Gruchy, Allan G. *Modern Economic Thought—the American Contribution*. New York: Prentice-Hall, Inc., 1947.

Gurvitch, Georges. *Sociology of Law*. London: K. Paul, Trench, Trubner and Co., Ltd., 1947.

———— and Wilbert E. Moore (eds.). *Twentieth Century Sociology*. New York: Philosophical Library, 1945. (Includes Roscoe Pound, "Sociology of Law," pp. 297–341.)

Hawley, Ellis W. *The New Deal and the Problem of Monopoly*. Princeton, N.J.: Princeton University Press, 1966.

Heilbroner, Robert L. *The Limits of American Capitalism*. New York: Harper & Row, 1965.

Hofstadter, Richard. *The Age of Reform*. New York: Vintage Books, 1955.

————. *The Progressive Historians*. New York: Alfred A. Knopf, 1968.

————. *Social Darwinism in American Thought*. Boston: Beacon Press, 1965.

Holmes, Oliver Wendell, Jr. *The Common Law*. Boston: Little, Brown & Co., 1923. First published in 1881.

Howe, Mark DeWolfe (ed.). *The Holmes-Pollock Letters,* vol. II. Cambridge: Harvard University Press, 1941.

Jandy, Edward C. *Charles Horton Cooley: His Life and Social Theory*. New York: Dryden Press, 1942.

Key, V. O. *Public Opinion and American Democracy*. New York: Alfred A. Knopf, 1961.

Lane, Robert E. and David O. Sears. *Public Opinion*. Englewood Cliffs, N.J.: Prentice-Hall, Inc., 1964.

Lasswell, Harold D. *Politics—Who Gets What, When, How*. New York: McGraw-Hill, 1936.

————. *Psychopathology and Politics*. Chicago: University of Chicago Press, 1930.

————. *World Politics and Personal Insecurity*. Chicago: University of Chicago Press, 1934.

Le Buffe, Francis and James Hayes. *The American Philosophy of Law*. New York: Crusader Press, 1947.

Lerner, Max. *The Mind and Faith of Justice Holmes*. New York: Modern Library, 1943.

Lewis, Anthony. *Gideon's Trumpet*. New York: Random House, 1964.

Llewellyn, Karl N. *Jurisprudence—Realism in Theory and Practice*. Chicago: University of Chicago Press, 1962.

Mason, Alpheus T. *The Brandeis Way*. Princeton, N.J.: Princeton University Press, 1938.

Merriam, Charles E. *New Aspects of Politics*. Chicago: University of Chicago Press, 1925.

————. *The Role of Politics in Social Change*. New York: New York University Press, 1936.

————. *Systematic Politics*. Chicago: University of Chicago Press, 1945.

Mills, C. Wright (ed.). *Images of Man*. New York: George Braziller, Inc., 1960.

Monsen, R. Joseph and Mark W. Cannon. *The Makers of Public Policy—American Power Groups and Their Ideologies.* New York: McGraw-Hill, 1965.

Ogburn, William F. *On Culture and Social Change—Selected Papers,* edited by Otis Dudley Duncan. Chicago: University of Chicago Press, 1964.

Perry, Ralph Barton. *The Thought and Character of William James,* vol. II. Boston: Little, Brown & Co., 1935.

Pound, Roscoe. *Interpretations of Legal History.* New York: Macmillan, 1923.

Reuschlein, Harold G. *Jurisprudence—Its American Prophets.* Indianapolis: Bobbs-Merrill Company, Inc., 1951.

Robinson, Edward S. *Law and the Lawyers.* New York: Macmillan, 1937.

Ross, Edward A. *Civic Sociology: A Textbook in Social and Civic Problems for Young Americans.* New York: World Book Co., 1930. First published in 1925.

———. *Seventy Years of It.* New York: D. Appleton Century Co., 1936.

———. *Sin and Society.* Boston and New York: Houghton Mifflin Co., 1907.

———. *Social Control.* New York: Macmillan, 1929.

Sayre, Paul. *The Life of Roscoe Pound.* Iowa City: State University of Iowa Press, 1948.

Schlesinger, Arthur M., Jr. *The Age of Jackson.* Boston: Little, Brown & Co., 1945.

Smith, J. Allen. *The Spirit of American Government.* New York: Macmillan, 1907.

Stone, Julius. *Legal System and Lawyers' Reasonings.* Stanford, Calif.: Stanford University Press, 1964.

Tugwell, Rexford G. *The Democratic Roosevelt.* Garden City, N.Y.: Doubleday, 1957.

Twiss, Benjamin R. *Lawyers and the Constitution.* Princeton, N.J.: Princeton University Press, 1942.

Veblen, Thorstein. *Imperial Germany and the Industrial Revolution.* New York: Viking Press, 1954. First published in 1915.

———. *The Instinct of Workmanship.* New York: W. W. Norton and Co., 1964. First published in 1914.

———. *The Theory of Business Enterprise.* New York: Charles Scribner's Sons, 1904.

———. *The Theory of the Leisure Class.* New York: Modern Library, 1934. First published in 1899.

White, Leonard D. (ed.). *The Future of Government in the United States: Essays in Honor of Charles E. Merriam.* Chicago: University of Chicago Press, 1942. (Includes Charles E. Merriam, "The Education of Charles E. Merriam," pp. 1–24.)

White, Morton G. *The Origins of Dewey's Instrumentalism.* New York: Octagon Books, Inc., 1964. First published by Columbia University Press in 1943.

# Thurman Arnold, Social Critic

White, Morton G. *Social Thought in America—the Revolt Against Formalism*. Boston: Beacon Press, 1957.

Wiener, Philip P. *Evolution and the Founders of Pragmatism*. Cambridge: Harvard University Press, 1949.

## Articles

Alsop, Joseph and Robert Kintner. "Trustbuster: The Folklore of Thurman Arnold," *Saturday Evening Post*, vol. 212 (August 12, 1939), pp. 5–7, 30, 33–34.

Blake, Harlan M. and William K. Jones. "In Defense of Antitrust," *Columbia Law Review*, vol. 65 (March 1965), p. 381.

Bork, Robert H. and Ward S. Bowman. "The Crisis in Antitrust," *Columbia Law Review*, vol. 65 (March 1965), p. 363–76.

Boulding, Kenneth E. "The Knowledge Boom," *Challenge*, vol. 14 (July/August 1966), pp. 5–7.

———. "A New Look at Institutionalism," *American Economic Review—Papers and Proceedings*, vol. 47 (May 1957), pp. 1–12.

Burke, Kenneth. "The Virtues and Limitations of Debunking," *Southern Review*, vol. 3 (spring 1938), pp. 640–56.

Cassels, Louis. "Arnold, Fortas, Porter and Prosperity," *Harper's*, vol. 203 (November 1951), pp. 62–70.

Clark, Delbert. "Mr. Arnold Begs to Differ," *New York Times Magazine* (July 12, 1942), pp. 12, 20.

Clark, John Maurice. "Recent Developments in Economics," *Recent Developments in the Social Sciences*. Philadelphia: Lippincott, 1927, pp. 213–306.

Cooley, Charles H. "Political Economy and Social Process," *Sociological Theory and Social Research*. New York: Henry Holt, 1930, pp. 251–59.

Corwin, Edward S. "Review of the Folklore of Capitalism," *American Political Science Review*, vol. 32 (August 1938), pp. 745–46.

Dewey, Donald. "The Shaky Case for Antitrust," *Challenge*, vol. 14 (January/February 1966), p. 19.

Dewey, John. "Logical Method and Law," *Cornell Law Quarterly*, vol. 10 (December 1924), pp. 17–27.

Edwards, Corwin D. "Thurman Arnold and the Antitrust Laws," *Political Science Quarterly*, vol. 58 (September 1943), pp. 338–55.

Ellis, Ellen D. "Political Science at the Crossroads," *American Political Science Review*, vol. 21 (November 1927), pp. 773–91.

Featherstone, Joseph. "The Machiavelli of the New Deal," *New Republic*, vol. 153 (August 7, 1965), pp. 22–26.

Feldman, Myer. "On the Side of Law and a New Order," *Saturday Review*, vol. 48 (July 31, 1965), p. 19.

Fisch, M. H. "Justice Holmes, the Prediction Theory of Law, and Pragmatism," *Journal of Philosophy*, vol. 39 (1942), pp. 85–97.

Goldman, Eric F. and Mary Paull. "Liberals on Liberalism," *New Republic*, vol. 115 (July 22, 1946), pp. 70–73.

Hale, Myron Q. "The Cosmology of Arthur F. Bentley," *The American Political Science Review*, vol. 54 (December 1960), p. 958.

Hamilton, Walton H. "Charles Horton Cooley," *Social Forces*, vol. 8 (December 1929), pp. 183–87.

Hamilton, Walton H. and Irene Till. "Antitrust—the Reach after New Weapons," *Washington University Law Quarterly*, vol. 26 (December 1940), pp. 1–26.

Harberger, Arnold C. "Monopoly and Resource Allocation," *American Economic Review*, vol. 44 (May 1954), p. 84.

Hertzler, J. O. "Edward Alsworth Ross: Sociological Pioneer and Interpreter," *American Sociological Review*, vol. 16 (1951), pp. 597–613.

Hill, Forest G. "Wesley Mitchell's Theory of Planning," *Political Science Quarterly*, vol. 72 (1957), pp. 100–18.

Hill, Warren P. "The Psychological Realism of Thurman Arnold," *University of Chicago Law Review*, vol. 22 (winter 1955), pp. 377–96.

Holmes, Oliver W., Jr. "The Path of the Law," *Harvard Law Review*, vol. 10 (March 1897), pp. 460–61.

Hook, Sidney. "The Folklore of Capitalism: The Politician's Handbook—a Review," *University of Chicago Law Review*, vol. 5 (April 1938), pp. 341–49.

———. "Neither Myth nor Power—A Rejoinder," *University of Chicago Law Review*, vol. 5 (April 1938), pp. 354–57.

Hutton, William W. "Thurman Arnold: Protector of Consumer's Interests," *University of Kansas City Law Review*, vol. 14 (April–June 1946), pp. 69–105.

Lerner, Max. "The Shadow World of Thurman Arnold," *Yale Law Journal*, vol. 47 (March 1938), pp. 687–703.

Llewellyn, Karl N. "Some Realism About Realism," *Harvard Law Review*, vol. 44 (June 1931), pp. 1222–64.

Moley, Raymond. "Last of the Jongleurs," *Newsweek*, vol. 11 (February 28, 1938), p. 44.

———. "Wrong Way Arnold," *Newsweek*, vol. 12 (November 28, 1938), p. 44.

Perlman, Selig. "John Rogers Commons: 1862–1945," *Wisconsin Magazine of History*, vol. 29 (September 1945), pp. 25–31.

Reich, Charles A. "Individual Rights and Social Welfare: The Emerging Legal Issues," *Yale Law Journal*, vol. 74 (June 1965), pp. 1245–57.

Rheinstein, Max. "The Role of Reason in Politics—According to Thurman Arnold," *Ethics*, vol. 49 (January 1939), pp. 212–17.

Rostow, Eugene V. "A Combative Life Devoted to Ridiculing Unreality," *Life*, vol. 59 (July 9, 1965), p. 10.

Rumble, Wilfred E. "Legal Realism, Sociological Jurisprudence and Mr. Justice Holmes," *Journal of the History of Ideas*, vol. 26, pp. 547–66.

Schwartzman, David. "The Effect of Monopoly on Price," *Journal of Political Economy,* vol. 67 (August 1959), pp. 360–61.

Stern, Bernhard J. "The Ward-Ross Correspondence 1891–96," *American Sociological Review,* vol. 3 (1938), pp. 362–401.

――――. "The Ward-Ross Correspondence II 1897–1901," *American Sociological Review,* vol. 11 (1946), pp. 593–605, 734–48.

――――. "The Ward-Ross Correspondence III 1904–1905," *American Sociological Review,* vol. 13 (1948), pp. 82–94.

Strout, Richard L. "The Folklore of Thurman Arnold," *New Republic,* vol. 106 (April 27, 1942), pp. 570–71.

Walker, Jack L. "A Critique of the Elitist Theory of Democracy," *American Political Science Review,* vol. 60 (June 1966), pp. 285–95.

### Unpublished Doctoral Dissertation

Titus, James E. "Studies in American Liberalism of the 1930's," Madison: University of Wisconsin, 1957.

### Other Cases Cited

*Abrams* v. *United States.* 250 U.S. 616 (1919).

*Buck* v. *Bell.* 274 U.S. 200 (1927).

*Dennis* v. *United States.* 341 U.S. 494, at 525.

*Durham* v. *United States.* 214 F. 2d, 862 (1954).

*Gideon* v. *Wainwright.* 372 U.S. 335 (1963).

*Gitlow* v. *New York.* 368 U.S. 652 (1925).

*Home Building and Loan Association* v. *Blaisdell.* 290 U.S. 398 (1934).

*Lochner* v. *New York.* 198 U.S. 45 (1905).

*Minersville School District* v. *Gobitis.* 310 U.S. 586 (1940).

*Nebbia* v. *New York.* 291 U.S. 502 (1934).

*Ryan* v. *Panama Refining Co.* 293 U.S. 388 (1935).

*Schechter Poultry Corp.* v. *United States.* 295 U.S. 495 (1935).

Scottsboro Cases: *Powell* v. *Alabama.* 278 U.S. 45 (1932). *Patterson* v. *Alabama* 294 U.S. 600 (1934).

*United States* v. *Aluminum Co. of America.* 44 F. Supp. 97 (1941); 148 F. 2d, 416, 431 (1945).

*United States* v. *American Medical Association.* 28 F. Supp. 752 (1939).

*United States* v. *Borden Co. et al.* 308 U.S. 188 (1939).

*United States* v. *Ethyl Gasoline Corp.* 309 U.S. 436 (1940).

*United States* v. *Paramount Pictures.* 70 F. Supp. 53 (1947); 334 U.S. 131 (1948).

# INDEX